Celebrity Lights

Celebrity Lights

A Collection of Favourite Recipes from Celebrity Women
in Support of Breast Cancer Research

Celebrity Lights Foundation
Nanaimo, British Columbia, Canada

WOMEN *to* WOMEN
A Gift of Hope

Canadian Cataloguing in Publication Data

Main entry under title:
    Celebrity lights

Includes index.
ISBN 0-9681159-0-X

    1. Cookery. I. Celebrity Lights Foundation

TX714.C44 1996   641.5   C96-900651-9

Project Co-ordinator   Donna Dash
Managing Editor & Writer   Lisa Leighton
Graphic Designer & Illustrator   Valerie Luedke
Digital Pre-press Co-ordinator   Mary-Jane Jessen
Researcher & Proofreader   Jean MacDonald
Photographer   Kim Stallknecht
Food Stylist   Deborah Melanson

First Printing - 1996
Printed in Canada by Hemlock Printers Ltd., Burnaby, British Columbia,
on Luna stock from Island Paper Mills Co. Ltd., New Westminster, British Columbia.

Celebrity Lights is dedicated to women everywhere who have lost their lives to breast cancer.

Message from the Canadian Cancer Society

We are taken with the creativity and beauty of Celebrity Lights. *The incredible drive and passion of Donna Dash, the catalyst for this project, and the generosity and effort of all those who have worked on this book, is truly inspiring. It is heartwarming to see people from all walks of life come together to support such an important cause.*

We wish to assure you that the money raised from this project will go to the best breast cancer research existing today, and that this research, step by step, is already making a difference in the lives of women living with breast cancer.

Holly Davidson
Chair-Elect
National Revenue Development Committee
Canadian Cancer Society

There are two ways of spreading light:
to be the candle or the mirror that reflects it.

Edith Wharton

Acknowledgements

First and foremost, we thank the celebrities, the 96 wonderful, caring women who so readily and willingly agreed to be a part of *Celebrity Lights*. Without them, this book wouldn't exist. These generous women, in most cases without knowing who else was participating, responded to our invitation because they believed in the cause. For that, we are most grateful.

Our Project Committee is another outstanding team of women, and they deserve a great deal of credit for their dedication in bringing the dream to life. Thank you to Valerie Luedke, Lisa Leighton, Kim Stallknecht, Deborah Melanson, Cora Wilson, Lucie Gosselin, Shelley Chase and Carrie Crowe. *Celebrity Lights* is a combination of their own unique and special talents.

Thank you, also, to Mary-Jane Jessen and Jean MacDonald, and to so many others who have helped, including our sponsors, all of the participating shopping centres, and the retailers who are selling the books. Although many of them are competitors, they are working together for this project without any financial profit. Special thanks to Don Kraushar of Overwaitea Foods for his early and solid support. It's easy to get behind something when it's a proven success, but not everyone is willing to take a chance on "an idea." Don had the vision to do that.

On behalf of the entire production team, thanks to our families for their support and encouragement.

Finally, we thank you for supporting breast cancer research by purchasing this book. Enjoy!

Donna Dash
President
Celebrity Lights Foundation

Introduction

Welcome to *Celebrity Lights*, a fundraising initiative that has captured the attention and the hearts of nearly a hundred national and international celebrities – prominent women from almost every field of endeavour, from four different countries and three continents!

Most of the women featured in this book are widely known and will be recognized immediately. Every one of them is a celebrity in every sense of the word. A wonderful *sidelight* of this project is that it recognizes many of Canada's most talented, highly accomplished women, including some who don't normally find themselves in the *limelight*.

Because breast cancer knows no geographic borders, we felt that it was important to invite celebrities everywhere to participate. We were pleased and proud to hear from so many Canadians, thrilled when a number of American women joined in, and ecstatic when recipes arrived from Britain and The Philippines.

Light is hope, and that is what this book is about. *Celebrity Lights* is a beautiful collection of recipes, and it is also a gift of hope from women to women in the fight against breast cancer. The gift is precious, yet powerful, and it carries a message that is clear: **women care about this issue**. They want to do something about it and will work together to help one another. As you read through the book, you'll discover just how special it is. The incredible women who are featured within these pages have not only shared a favourite recipe – and there are some great selections – but many have also shared a part of themselves. The personal glimpses, anecdotes and good wishes are both inspirational and emotional.

Two years ago, a personal breast cancer scare left me with the desire to do something positive to help in the battle against this dreaded disease. I truly believed that women everywhere shared this concern and, by joining together, we could make a difference. In my career as a shopping centre marketing director, I also saw *Celebrity Lights* as a way for those in the retail industry to give back to their customers and communities. This is how the shopping centres and retailers became involved. Having a means to distribute and sell the book was also an integral part of its overall success.

We encourage women to purchase *Celebrity Lights* for themselves and to buy the books as gifts. The spirit of "women to women" will carry on in the giving and sharing of books between friends and loved ones.

We also invite men to buy this book. Of course! Not only will they appreciate the recipes, but more importantly, they too are touched by the devastating effects of breast cancer, and they too support this cause. No family is immune. In fact, many men have helped to make *Celebrity Lights* a reality.

We hope you will all enjoy *Celebrity Lights* as much as we have enjoyed producing it.

Donna Dash
Nanaimo, British Columbia, Canada
1996

Table of Contents

The Book

The Lights

Morning Light

Sunlight

Tea Lights

Highlights

Twilight

Candlelight

14

Firelight

Inner Light

The Project

About the Recipes

Our "lights" recipe categories were created to reflect the theme of *Celebrity Lights*. With a very few exceptions, they are certainly not definitive. Aline Chrétien's Meat Pie, for example, is a classic morning dish in Québec, but for many it also has an honoured place at the dinner table, especially during the Christmas season. Feel free to move these recipes, like candles, to create new lights among your own traditions.

Our "light" theme is also strictly aesthetic, not medical or scientific. While net proceeds from sales of *Celebrity Lights* will go to support breast cancer research, this book is not a diet or a collection of recipes assembled for the prevention or treatment of any disease, including breast cancer. Questions about diet and health, especially with respect to illness, should be directed to a physician. Nor are the recipes contained in this book necessarily "light" insofar as fat or carbohydrate content. Celebrity Lights Foundation is publishing *Celebrity Lights* for the sole reason of raising money for breast cancer research.

Some of these recipes arrived handwritten in rumpled envelopes, and some arrived typeset on the latest digital equipment. Regardless of how they came, we have made every effort to accurately and faithfully reproduce them in every detail. In some submissions, measurements have been estimated, because many old family favourites never had quantities written down. So if you find that a particular measure doesn't work for you, adjust the quantity and try again. After all, that's usually how our own most treasured recipes evolve.

Abbreviations are used for most measurements throughout *Celebrity Lights* to conserve space and improve ease of reading. These are the standard abbreviations:

tsp	teaspoon	oz	ounce
tbsp	tablespoon	lb	pound
pkg	package	qt	quart

Metric Conversions

All measurements in *Celebrity Lights* are Imperial and/or conventional. Standard metric equivalents are provided below.

Metric measures do not always exactly equal conventional measures, so in some cases, metrics have been rounded up or down (e.g., 1/4 cup = 56.8 millilitres, rounded down to a standard 50 millilitres). Exact metric measures are shown in brackets where numbers have been rounded up or down by more than 5.

The benchmark for this book is 1 cup (8 fluid ounces or 16 tablespoons) = 250 millilitres.

Liquid

1/4 teaspoon	1 millilitre
1/2 teaspoon	2 millilitres
1 teaspoon	5 millilitres
1-1/2 teaspoons	7 millilitres
2 teaspoons	10 millilitres (9.4)
1 tablespoon	15 millilitres (14.2)
1/4 cup (4 tbsp)	50 millilitres (56.8)
1/3 cup (5-1/3 tbsp)	75 millilitres
1/2 cup (8 tbsp)	125 millilitres (113.6)
2/3 cup	150 millilitres
3/4 cup (12 tbsp)	175 millilitres
1 cup (16 tbsp)	250 millilitres (227.2)
4 cups (1 quart)	900 millilitres (908.8)
4-1/2 cups	1000 millilitres, 1 litre (1022.4)

Pans

8-inch x 2-inch round	20 cm x 5 cm
9-inch x 2-inch round	22 cm x 5 cm
8-inch by 8-inch	20 cm x 20 cm
9-inch by 9-inch	22 cm x 22 cm
9-inch x 13-inch	22 cm x 33 cm

Weight

1 ounce	30 grams
1-1/2 ounces	45 grams
2 ounces	55 grams
3 ounces	85 grams
4 ounces	125 grams (113.4)
5 ounces	140 grams
6 ounces	170 grams
7 ounces	200 grams
8 ounces	250 grams (226.8)
10 ounces	280 grams
16 ounces	500 grams (453.6)
32 ounces	900 grams (907.2)
35 ounces	1000 grams, 1 kilogram (992.2)

Temperatures (all degrees)

Fahrenheit	Celsius	Fahrenheit	Celsius
175	80	350	180
200	100	375	190
225	110	400	200
250	120	425	220
275	140	450	230
300	150	475	240
325	160	500	260

You gain strength, courage and confidence by every
experience in which you
really stop to look fear in the face.
You must do the thing which you think you cannot do.

Eleanor Roosevelt

I am only one; but still I am one.
I cannot do everything, but still
I can do something; I will not refuse
to do the something I can do.

Helen Keller

Morning Light

Favourites for breakfasts, brunches and coffee-breaks

WOMEN *to* WOMEN

A Gift of Hope

Meat Pie

1 lb ground pork
1 onion, finely chopped
1 tsp poultry seasoning
salt and pepper to taste
1 small potato, cubed

pastry for a 2-crust
9-inch pie
(or pastry for 6
individual 2-inch
pies)

Combine all ingredients and cover with water. Simmer for 1-1/2 hours. Drain, and reserve liquid.

With a fork, mash cooked mixture to an even consistency.

Pour into unbaked pie shell. Sprinkle some of the reserved liquid onto the mixture. Cover with pie crust.

Bake at 350°F for approximately 30 minutes, or until crust is golden.

Bon appétit!

Peter Caton/Gerald Campbell Studios

Aline Chrétien

*Wife of the Rt. Hon.
Jean Chrétien, Prime Minister
of Canada,*
Ottawa, Ontario, Canada

WOMEN to WOMEN
A Gift of Hope

Ice Box Rolls

"This is a roll recipe used by my aunt since her marriage in 1944, and a favourite with my family. Everyone from the South likes hot bread, and this is a very easy recipe and can be used for many things."

Bruce Davidson

1/2 cup milk	1/2 cup cold water
1 tsp salt	1 yeast cake
2 tbsp sugar	flour to thicken
1/3 cup shortening	1 egg

Mix milk, salt, sugar and shortening. Heat until shortening melts. Pour into a bowl and let cool.

Add the cold water. Dissolve the yeast cake and add. Add flour until the mixture is as thick as waffle batter. Add the egg and beat. Add more flour until you have a thick dough. Set in a warm place and let rise.

After it has risen, take the dough out of the bowl, put it on a floured surface and roll it out. Cut with a round cutter. Fold over each roll and stick together with a little shortening (I use Crisco). Let rise again.

Place rolls on ungreased cookie sheet and bake in a 375°F oven until lightly browned.

Unused dough may be covered and kept several days in the refrigerator.

This dough may also be used to make cinnamon buns, or a cinnamon ring roll.

Joanne Woodward

Actress
Stamford, Connecticut, U.S.A.

Ice Box Rolls are pictured on page 121.

WOMEN *to* WOMEN
A Gift of Hope

Wild Rice Muffins

"The muffins are moist and nutty – ideal for a special brunch. They feature one of Canada's premier homegrown products – wild rice."

1/3 cup wild rice

2 eggs

1 cup milk

1/2 cup butter, melted and cooled

1-1/2 cups all-purpose flour

1/2 cup natural bran

1/3 cup packed brown sugar

1 tbsp baking powder

1/4 tsp salt

1/4 tsp nutmeg

1/2 cup chopped toasted pecans

1/2 cup sliced dates

1/4 cup slivered apricots

2 tsp coarsely grated orange rind

To toast pecans, bake on a baking sheet in a 350°F oven for 5 to 10 minutes or until golden.

In a small saucepan, bring 2 cups water to a boil. Add rice, cover and cook over medium heat until very tender and splayed, about 45 minutes. Drain well and let cool.

In a bowl, whisk eggs. Mix in rice, milk and butter.

WOMEN to WOMEN
A Gift of Hope

In a large bowl, stir together flour, bran, sugar, baking powder, salt and nutmeg. Pour in the rice mixture. Sprinkle with pecans, dates, apricots and orange rind. Mix together just until dry ingredients are moistened.

Spoon batter into large, paper-lined muffin cups, filling each to top of liner. Bake in a 375°F oven for about 25 minutes, or until golden and firm to the touch.

Makes 10 large muffins.

Elizabeth Baird

Food Director, Canadian Living Magazine
Toronto, Ontario, Canada

"I have had the privilege of meeting many Canadians in the food world. I am pleased to share their knowledge with Canadian Living *readers, and I am always delighted to contribute to a cause to help other people."*

Gingerbread Pancakes

1-1/4 cups whole wheat
  flour

1 tsp baking soda

2/3 tsp ground ginger

2/3 tsp ground
  cinnamon

1/3 tsp ground cloves

pinch salt

1 tbsp instant
  decaffeinated coffee
  powder

1/3 cup hot water

1 cup frozen apple juice
  concentrate, thawed

3 tbsp margarine,
  melted

1 large egg, beaten

Combine flour, baking soda, ginger, cinnamon, cloves and salt in a large mixing bowl.

In a smaller bowl, dissolve the instant coffee in the hot water. Add apple juice concentrate and melted margarine, and mix well.

Add the liquid ingredients to the dry ingredients and mix just enough to moisten the dry ingredients. The mixture will be lumpy.

Spray a hot skillet or griddle with non-stick vegetable coating. Pour the batter, 2 tbsp at a time, onto the griddle. Cook until the top of each pancake is covered with tiny bubbles, and the bottom is brown. Turn and brown the other side.

Makes 24 pancakes.

Mila Mulroney

*Business woman and wife of
the Rt. Hon. Brian Mulroney,
former Prime Minister
of Canada*
Montréal, Québec, Canada

*"By working together we will come
closer to finding a cure
for breast cancer."*

WOMEN to WOMEN
A Gift of Hope

Easter Bread

1/2 cup sugar

1 tsp salt

1/2 cup butter

1-1/4 cups milk

2 yeast cakes

5 cups flour

4 eggs, beaten

1 tbsp grated orange rind

1 tbsp grated lemon rind

1/2 cup chopped almonds

1 cup raisins

Scald the milk. Pour over sugar and butter. Cool (until warm).

Dissolve the yeast with a little of the warm milk mixture, and add it back to the remaining milk mixture. Add half of the flour and beat well.

Add salt to eggs and beat until thick. Add the eggs to the main batter and mix well. Add orange rind, lemon rind, almonds and raisins. Knead for 15 minutes.

Cover and let rise until double in bulk. Place in a well-buttered tube pan and brush the top with an egg yolk-water mixture. Bake for 35 to 45 minutes in a 350°F oven. *Do not overbake.*

Heather Dean

Cecilia Walters

Canadian Broadcasting Corporation radio broadcaster
Vancouver, British Columbia, Canada

"From a woman, for women. What a great idea."

Far away up there in the sunshine are my
highest aspirations.
I may not reach them, but I can look up and
see their beauty, believe in them,
and try to follow where they lead.

Louisa May Alcott

Just don't give up trying to do what you
really want to do. Where there is
love and inspiration, I don't
think you can go wrong.

Ella Fitzgerald

Sunlight

Midday recipes for hot and cold lunches

Curried Carrot Soup

"I love this soup because you can make it as spicy as your mood wants or needs."

1/4 cup butter

1 medium onion, chopped

2 - 3 tsp curry powder

10 large carrots, peeled and sliced

4 cubes chicken bouillon

6 cups water

dash nutmeg

3 tbsp sherry

salt and pepper to taste

chopped chives for garnish

Melt butter in a large saucepan. Over low heat, sauté onion with curry until soft. Add remaining ingredients and bring to a boil. Simmer until carrots are tender.

Using a blender or food processor, purée the soup. Reheat. Garnish with chopped chives and serve immediately.

Enjoy.

Sonja Smits

Actor and star of the television series Street Legal *and* Traders
Toronto, Ontario, Canada

WOMEN *to* WOMEN
A Gift of Hope

Borscht

1-1/2 cups diced
    potatoes

2-1/2 cups diced beets

1 tsp salt

1 tbsp vinegar

1 cup sliced carrots

1 cup 1-inch string beans

1 cup green peas

2 cups shredded cabbage

1 tbsp chopped parsley

1 tbsp chopped dill leaves

1/4 cup chopped onion

1 qt tomatoes, peeled
    and quartered

1 stalk celery, diced

salt and pepper to taste

1/2 cup chopped onion

1/3 cup butter

1-1/2 tsp chopped
    dill leaves

1 tbsp sugar

1 cup sour cream

Ann Elliott-Cutting

Cover potatoes and beets with water, and add salt
and vinegar. Bring to a boil and add carrots,
beans and peas. Add enough water to cover the
vegetables and boil for 15 minutes. Add the
shredded cabbage, parsley, 1 tbsp of chopped dill,
1/4 cup of chopped onions, tomatoes, celery, salt
and pepper. Add more water if necessary.

Sauté the 1/2 cup of chopped onions in butter
until tender but not brown. Add to the soup
with 1-1/2 tsp of chopped dill and 1 tbsp of
sugar. Boil for 10 minutes. Mix well and allow to
rest for 30 minutes.

Add a little of the soup broth to the sour cream,
then add it all to the soup. Stir well.
Simmer on low heat for a
few minutes until heated
through.

Loreena McKennitt

Singer and songwriter
Stratford, Ontario, Canada

*"I am pleased to support this
worthwhile endeavour, as no family,
including my own, is immune to the
devastating effects of cancer."*

WOMEN to WOMEN
A Gift of Hope

29

Black and White Bean Soup

"You can use canned black and white beans for this soup, and it's really easy, tasty and low-fat! All the juices add complexity to the flavour."

1/3 cup chopped onion

3-1/2 cups chicken stock (preferably homemade)

3 cloves fresh garlic, minced

1 large carrot, chopped

1 stalk celery, chopped

1 tsp ground coriander

1 tsp ground cumin

1 can black beans

1 can cannelini beans OR great northern beans

1/2 cup orange juice, freshly squeezed

1/4 cup dry sherry

1/4 tsp pepper, freshly ground

1/4 tsp cayenne pepper (optional)

1/2 tsp lemon juice

1/2 cup apple juice

freshly chopped cilantro for garnish

WOMEN to WOMEN
A Gift of Hope

Place the onion and 1/2 cup of the stock in a heavy soup pot and bring to a boil. Lower the heat and simmer, stirring, until the onion becomes soft and transparent. Then stir in the garlic, carrot and celery. Cook 5 minutes over medium heat, stirring occasionally. Add coriander and cumin, and cook an additional 5 minutes. If the mixture dries out, add more stock as needed.

Add the black beans, remaining stock, orange juice and sherry, and let cook for 20 minutes over medium heat, covered, stirring occasionally. Add the peppers, lemon juice and apple juice. Taste and adjust seasonings. Put half of the soup in a blender to make a thick purée. (As an option, you can open a can of refried beans and use them as needed to thicken the soup.) Add back to the pot. Garnish with cilantro.

Kathy Mattea

Recording artist
Nashville, Tennessee, U.S.A.

Cream of Cauliflower Soup

"This recipe is my specialty. I know it's not so light, but I am curious about a lighter version. It has always tasted good."

2 large onions	4 cups cold water
3 stalks celery	1 pkg onion soup mix (I use Knorr)
1/4 cup butter	1 large head (or 2 small heads) cauliflower
1/4 cup flour	

I'm not entirely consistent on this part ... I use whatever is in the fridge. I'll describe a recent variation:

1 tsp curry paste	1 tsp honey mustard
a few shakes dried hot chili peppers	cereal bowl-full grated cheddar cheese
1/2 tsp nutmeg	OR 3/4 cup grated parmesan cheese
2 soup spoons red cooking wine or real wine	2 cubes or pkgs instant bouillon (chicken or vegetable)
6 turns of pepper from grinder	2 cups water
a few shakes curry powder	2 cups cream

WOMEN to WOMEN
A Gift of Hope

In a huge pot, sauté the onions and celery in the butter. Stir in the flour until it's a pasty consistency. Add the cold water and package of onion soup mix. Set the stove to medium-low.

Stem cauliflower head(s) – *do not precook*. Finely grind 2/3 of the cauliflower through a food processor and add to the pot. Chop by hand the other 1/3 of the cauliflower into small chunks and set aside.

As the soup warms, add the flavouring (from the curry paste to the cheese).

Then add the bouillon cubes or powder and the water, and stir in the remaining 1/3 of the cauliflower.

After about 30 minutes, add the cream and reduce the heat to low. Most people dislike crock-pot cooking, but I have a minute kitchen. When there's 1 hour until mealtime, I transfer the soup to the crock pot and let it stay warm on low until dinner.

I serve the soup as an appetizer with garlic bread.

Serves 6 to 8.

Phillip Smith

Sara Craig

Singer and painter
Toronto, Ontario, Canada

"I'm so excited for you, and thrilled to be a part of the project."

Hon. Alexa McDonough, MP

*Member of Parliament and
Leader of the
New Democratic Party of Canada*
Halifax, Nova Scotia, Canada

*"Thank you for bringing hope to
thousands of women."*

*Alexa McDonough's
Spinach Soup*

"Quick and easy!"

1 pkg frozen chopped
   spinach
OR fresh spinach

1 small onion

1 can (10 oz)
   chicken-rice soup

3 tbsp lemon juice

salt and pepper to taste

dash nutmeg

1 can (5-1/2 oz)
   evaporated milk

1 cup light cream

1-1/2 cups plain yogurt

sprinkle of paprika

Cook the spinach, but don't drain it.

Sauté the onion. Combine the spinach and onion with the other ingredients except the paprika, and heat through. If thick, add milk. Sprinkle with paprika.

Alexa McDonough's Spinach Soup is pictured on page 35.

WOMEN *to* WOMEN
A Gift of Hope

Halloween Soup, lower left, from Cassandra Peterson. See page 43.
Alexa McDonough's Spinach Soup, upper right. See page 34.
Indonesian Squash Soup, lower right, from Sarah McLachlan. See page 40.

Haricots verts à tarragon vinaigrette, foreground, from Dini Petty. See page 67.
Great, Low-Fat, Delicious, Almost-Roasted Potatoes, upper left, from Valerie Pringle. See page 82.
Turnip Puff, upper right, from Dr. Sylvia Fedoruk. See page 70.

Marjorie Harris's Romantic Pink Soup

"It's easy, healthy, and tastes absolutely divine."

1 container low-fat yogurt

1 can low-sodium chicken stock

1 can whole beets, chopped into small pieces

2 green onions, chopped fine (including the green part, or add some chives as well)

1 stalk celery, chopped fine

1/2 English cucumber, peeled and chopped fine (leave some peel on for colour)

some stock or water, if necessary

dill, chopped fine, for garnish

Mix the beet juice with the yogurt and chicken stock, then add the chopped beets. Add the remaining ingredients. The mixture should sit for a couple of hours for the flavours to blend.

I like to add some chopped shrimp or ham or smoked turkey to make it a lunch meal, with a really good, crisp bread and salad.

Malcolm Tweedy

Marjorie Harris

Editor, Toronto Life Gardens *magazine*
Toronto, Ontario, Canada

"I have had cancer twice. My mother died of cancer. I take it very seriously, but it has not banished my great love of just being alive, it has enhanced the joy."

WOMEN to WOMEN
A Gift of Hope

Michael Lavine/FOX

Frances Fisher

Stage, television and movie actress, and star of the television series Strange Luck
Los Angeles, California, U.S.A.

Frances Fisher's Gazpacho Soup

"No matter what the temperature is outside, this soup, served at room temperature, will warm you up."

6 ripe, medium tomatoes, blanched and peeled

1 medium onion, quartered

1 medium cucumber, peeled, seeded and quartered

2 cloves garlic

1/2 tsp salt

1/4 tsp black pepper

3 dashes Tabasco sauce

1 tbsp extra virgin olive oil

Place all ingredients in a blender, and pulse until almost smooth. Serve at room temperature.

Makes 2 generous servings.

WOMEN *to* WOMEN
A Gift of Hope

Very Fabulous Curried Apple Soup

"This is my favourite recipe because it is easy and delicious, and the whole family demands it every Christmas and Thanksgiving (also birthdays and Saturdays with an R)."

4 tbsp butter

1 large onion, coarsely chopped

2-1/2 cups chicken stock

1 tbsp (or more) curry powder

2 tbsp cornstarch

2 egg yolks

2/3 cup heavy cream, hot

2 (or more) Granny Smith apples

salt and freshly ground black pepper to taste

juice of 1 lemon

watercress leaves for garnish

George Evanshuk

June Callwood

Journalist
Toronto, Ontario, Canada

Melt butter. Add chopped onion and cook until soft, but not brown. Stir in chicken stock (I use the canned variety) and curry powder. Add cornstarch mixed with a little water. Bring to a boil and then simmer for 8 minutes. Add egg yolks to hot cream, and stir gradually into hot soup.

Remove from fire immediately and transfer mixture to a blender with 1 or 2 apples (I use 2), peeled, cored and sliced. Blend until smooth, or pass through a fine sieve. Season to taste with salt and pepper. Chill.

Peel, core and dice (very small dices) remaining apple(s) and marinate in lemon juice to keep colour. Just before serving, stir in diced apple, and garnish with watercress leaves.

WOMEN *to* WOMEN
A Gift of Hope

39

Indonesian Squash Soup

Dennis Keeley

Sarah McLachlan

Singer and songwriter
Vancouver, British Columbia,
Canada

1 tsp coriander powder
or seeds

1 tsp cumin powder or
seeds

1 tsp turmeric powder

1/2 tsp chili powder

15 almond, macadamia
or pecan nuts

1 large red onion, diced

2 large cloves garlic

3 tbsp vegetable oil

2 - 3 tsp freshly grated
ginger root

1 tsp salt

2 cups water or vegetable
stock

1 can (14 oz) coconut
milk

4 cups peeled, cubed
butternut or acorn
squash (or part sweet
potatoes)

Mix together and grind the nuts and spices (except ginger and salt) so it is all powder.

In a soup pot, briefly sauté the onion and garlic in the oil. Add ginger and salt and continue to sauté until the onions are translucent. Add water (or stock) and ground-spice mixture to the pot and simmer for 5 minutes. Stir in coconut milk and squash, and gently simmer, uncovered, for about 40 minutes or until the squash is tender.

Transfer half the recipe at a time to a blender, and purée. It's good with a dollop of sour cream and a hearty spin of the pepper grinder.

Indonesian Squash Soup is pictured on page 35.

WOMEN *to* WOMEN
A Gift of Hope

Scotch Broth

"It hits the spot when I come in from speed-skating on the Rideau Canal on a cold winter's day."

8 cups water

1 lb lamb stew meat, cut into small pieces

1/2 cup pearl or pot barley

1 cup diced turnip

2 cups diced carrot

2 medium onions, chopped

2 leeks, white part only, sliced (optional)

2 cups shredded cabbage, packed

1/2 cup chopped celery

2 tsp salt

1/2 tsp pepper

1/4 tsp thyme

Put water, lamb and barley into a large saucepan. Bring to a boil. Cover and simmer 1 hour.

Add remaining ingredients. Bring to a boil again. Cover and simmer for about 30 minutes. This is a thick soup. If you prefer, thin with water. Check seasoning.

Makes about 12 cups.

Michael Bedford Photography

Hon. Flora MacDonald, OC, O.Ont.

Chair, International Development Research Centre, director of various companies and organizations, and former Member of Parliament
Ottawa, Ontario, Canada

WOMEN to WOMEN
A Gift of Hope

Nanny's Awesome Clam Chowder

"I grew up strong and healthy on this recipe, eating it three days a week for 16 years. This is a real down-home recipe from rural Nova Scotia, passed along to me by my grandmother three months before she died. Many people are familiar with the very thick, creamy clam chowder, but this light recipe is the real stuff!"

Andrew MacNaughlan

Holly Cole

Jazz diva
Toronto, Ontario, Canada

1 can clams
  (save the juice)
OR, preferably,
1 pint fresh clams,
  steamed (save the
  cooking water)
2 medium potatoes

1 medium white onion

1 stalk celery

1 pint milk

2 tbsp butter

sea salt and freshly
  ground black pepper
  to taste

Peel and dice potatoes and onions. Chop celery. Pour juice from clams over raw vegetables in a saucepan, and simmer, covered, until vegetables are tender. (Note: If fresh clams are used, juice must be strained for sand.) Add clams and milk. Heat slowly – *do not boil!!!* Add salt and pepper to taste.

WOMEN *to* WOMEN
A Gift of Hope

Halloween Soup

1 lb black beans

1 large onion, chopped

2 cloves garlic, diced

2 tbsp A1 Sauce

salt and cayenne pepper
  to taste

1 lb carrots, sliced into
  rounds

cilantro for garnish
  (optional)

David Goldner, © 1993 Queen "B" Productions

Rinse and soak beans for 6 hours or overnight.

Drain beans and empty into a large soup pot.
Add enough cold water to cover the beans by 2
to 3 inches. Bring to a boil and then skim off
any foam that rises to the surface.

Add garlic and onion. Lower heat and cook
until onions are soft, about 15 minutes.

Next, add A1 Sauce, and salt and cayenne
pepper to taste. Cook for about 1 hour.

Add carrots and continue cooking for another
30 minutes.

Garnish with cilantro, if desired, before serving.

Cassandra Peterson ("Elvira")

Actress and writer
Hollywood, California, U.S.A.

Halloween Soup is pictured on page 35.

WOMEN to WOMEN
A Gift of Hope

Camouflage Soup

"Hot or cold, Camouflage Soup is very slimming and very nutritious. I've been making it for years. The name comes from its colours."

1 lb carrots, peeled
1 lb fresh spinach,
washed very well
6 cups water for
steaming

chicken or vegetable
bouillon to taste
milk to taste (optional)
your favourite herbs and
spices

Camouflage Soup is a basic soup recipe that will accept almost any of your favourite herbs and spices, including dill, basil, Mexican oregano, Italian or Chinese spices, or curry flavourings. It's a very versatile dish.

Steam carrots until almost cooked. Remove a couple of spoonfuls with a slotted spoon and set aside to use later as garnish. Add spinach to steamer with remaining carrots, and steam together for another 5 to 10 minutes, until both are cooked.

Spoon carrots/spinach into a blender until it's half full. Fill with broth (and milk, if desired – see below) and herbs and spices. Liquefy. Pour the liquefied mixture into a large bowl. Repeat with the remaining batch(es) of steamed carrots/spinach.

If you serve the soup cold, chill it for at least 2 hours. Hot or cold, just before serving, add some of the steamed carrots that were set aside as garnish.

Variations

You can add skim, 2%, whole or evaporated milk to the soup before blending, or after (stir well). For thicker soup, add your choice of cooked rice, cooked and cubed potatoes, or cooked corn. You can also thicken the soup by adding sour cream or yogurt.

Denise Grant

Buffy Sainte-Marie

Recording artist, visual artist and educator
Kauai, Hawaiian Islands, U.S.A.

WOMEN *to* WOMEN
A Gift of Hope

Spicy Salmon Mold

"A light, fresh summer dish. This uses up the leftovers from poached pink salmon, and looks very pretty and celebratory. It is adapted from Benoit's recipe, 'Scottish Molded Salmon'. I made a mistake in assembling it when I first made it, and like my version better!"

Make the day before serving.

2 cups (about) cooked salmon (skin and bones removed)

1 envelope Knox gelatin

1/4 cup cold water

1 cup light mayonnaise

3 tsp Dijon mustard

1 tsp medium Madras curry powder (use more or less if you have only mild or hot)

black olives, cherry tomatoes and English cucumber slices for garnish

Monica Hughes

Children's writer
Edmonton, Alberta, Canada

"I write to entertain, to return a sense of wonder to the reader, to stimulate the imagination, and, perhaps along the way, to increase awareness of our relationships with each other and with our fragile planet."

Flake salmon into even-sized pieces, but do not mash. Set aside.

Soak the gelatin in the cold water until it is soft. Then melt it over hot water and mix thoroughly with the mayonnaise, mustard and curry powder. Add the salmon. Press into an oiled small mold or pudding basin. Cover and refrigerate.

The next day, unmold the salmon onto a serving dish and surround with olives, tomatoes and slices of cucumber.

Curry Rice Salad

Source: "My Mom."

Salad

4 cups cooked rice, cold

1 shredded green pepper

2 tbsp shredded red pepper

1/2 - 3/4 cup raisins, pre-soaked

1/4 cup chopped parsley

2 tbsp chopped spring onion

Combine ingredients and toss.

Dressing

1/2 cup olive oil

4 tbsp white wine vinegar

1 tbsp lemon juice

1 clove garlic, mashed

1/2 tbsp sugar

1 - 1-1/2 tsp curry powder

salt and pepper to taste

Mix dressing thoroughly. Stir into salad and chill.

Garnish with salad greens, red and green pepper rings, and parsley flowers.

Gillian Anderson

Actress, and star of the television series **The X-Files**
Vancouver, British Columbia, Canada

Curry Rice Salad is pictured on page 102.

WOMEN to WOMEN
A Gift of Hope

Santa Fe Salad

"Low-fat and tastes great!"

Dressing

1/4 cup olive oil

juice of 2 limes

1/4 cup chopped
  cilantro

1 tsp cumin

salt and freshly ground
  pepper to taste

Salad

1 can (19 oz) black
  beans (turtle beans),
  rinsed and drained

1 diced red bell pepper

1 can (12 oz) kernel
  corn, drained

1/3 cup chopped red
  onion

1 jalapeño pepper,
  seeded and minced

In a medium bowl, whisk together oil and lime juice. Add cilantro, cumin, salt and pepper, and mix well. Stir in salad ingredients and correct the seasoning. Serve at room temperature.

Serves 6 to 8.

The Best of Bridge Women:

Karen Brimacombe, Mary Halpen, Linda Jacobson, Helen Miles, Val Robinson, Joan Wilson

Authors and publishers of
The Best of Bridge *cookbook series*
Calgary, Alberta, Canada

"Take six enthusiastic women, add talented tastebuds, a lively sense of humour, a good idea, and what do you get? Culinary chaos, a lot of laughter, and six best-selling cookbooks. This is one of our favourites from our newest cookbook, That's Trump, *published in the fall of 1995.*

"Congratulations on a wonderful idea."

WOMEN *to* WOMEN
A Gift of Hope

47

Cottage Cheese Salad

Vanna White

"Wheel of Fortune" game-show hostess
Beverly Hills, California, U.S.A.

1 box (3 oz) Jell-O (I use lime-flavoured)

1 container (32 oz) plain cottage cheese

1 can (8 oz) crushed pineapple

1 container (8 oz) Cool Whip whipped topping (regular or light)

In a bowl, put cottage cheese and pour the dry Jell-O mix over it, right from the box. Mix well. Drain pineapple, then add it to the mixture. Fold in Cool Whip. Refrigerate until ready to serve.

You can also add chopped walnuts or pecans, if desired.

WOMEN to WOMEN
A Gift of Hope

Grated Carrot, Daikon and Almond Salad

"Daikon is a Japanese horseradish (looks like a big, white carrot) and I usually buy it in Chinatown or at health food stores that carry fresh produce. It is quite mild, and an excellent blood cleanser.

"I make this salad when I have been too busy to eat well, and want something clean. I will eat a bowl of this as my whole meal. I swear this salad makes me feel great right away! Very vital and pleasing, and the nuts fill you up. Nature's garden dee-luxe!"

Andrew MacNaughtan

Salad

grated carrots

grated daikon

chopped green onions

whole almonds
  (I prefer raw)

fresh herbs, chopped fine
  (mint, cilantro,
  parsley, etc.)

Dressing

olive oil

lemon

fresh garlic, chopped fine
  (I use lots!)

cayenne pepper

dried tarragon

Jane Siberry

Singer, songwriter, recording artist and President of Sheeba Records
Toronto, Ontario, Canada

"Best wishes and good luck with your book."

Use whatever you have in the fridge or garden (e.g., Replace green onions with chives? Flax oil instead of olive? Basil instead of mint? Red cabbage instead of daikon?). Mix colours to suit yourself: too orange? Add more daikon. Use organic ingredients wherever possible.

A great variation

Add a few caraway seeds and some feta cheese.

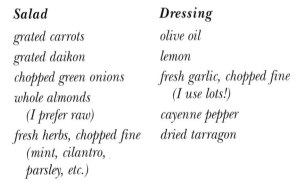

WOMEN *to* WOMEN
A Gift of Hope

Apple-Cinnamon Cabbage Salad

"The apples and cinnamon add a unique, sweet flavour, and the bicoloured apples and cabbage make the salad pretty enough to serve at a dinner party."

1/2 small head red cabbage, finely shredded

1/2 small head green cabbage, finely shredded

1 small sweet red apple, chopped into bite-sized chunks

1 small tart green apple, chopped into bite-sized chunks

3 tbsp brown rice vinegar or apple cider vinegar

3 tbsp vegetable oil (canola, safflower or sunflower)

2 tsp honey

1 tsp ground cinnamon

1/4 tsp ground marjoram

Garnish options:

1/2 cup chopped toasted pecans*

fresh parsley, chopped

*If you need to reduce the fat and calorie content, omit the pecans; if you don't, they're a nice addition.

WOMEN to WOMEN
A Gift of Hope

In a medium bowl, combine the shredded cabbage and apple chunks.

In a small bowl, whisk together the vinegar, oil, honey, cinnamon and marjoram. Pour over the cabbage and apples, and toss well.

Garnish with the pecans and parsley. Chill until ready to serve.

Serves 4 to 6.

Substitutions

All green or all red cabbage can be used here instead of the mix.

Cherie M. Calbom, MS, CN

Author, Certified Nutritionist, Master of Science in Nutrition, Member of the Society for Nutrition Education and the American College of Nutrition

Santa Fe, New Mexico, U.S.A.

"*My mother died of breast cancer when I was six years old, so I have a strong interest in helping women prevent cancer. I have written a book entitled* Nutrition and Cancer, *I devoted a chapter to cancer in my book* Juicing for Life, *and I designed a cancer-prevention menu plan along with dozens of nutribites about cancer prevention in my latest cookbook,* The Healthy Gourmet.*"*

51

If you don't experience your life, you're not going to
come up with solutions for anything.
Every intention, every achievement
has come out of dissatisfaction, not serenity.
No one ever said,
"Things are perfect. Let's invent fire."

Fran Lebowitz

The only thing that makes life possible is permanent,

intolerable uncertainty; not knowing what comes next.

Ursula K. LeGuin

Life is a do-it-yourself kit.

Phyllis Diller

Tea Lights

Sweet afternoon delights

WOMEN *to* WOMEN
A Gift of Hope

Hillary Clinton's Chocolate Chip Cookies

Courtesy Times Colonist

Hillary Clinton

Lawyer and First Lady of the United States of America
Washington, D.C., U.S.A.

1-1/2 cups unsifted all-purpose flour

1 tsp salt

1 tsp baking soda

1 cup solid vegetable shortening

1 cup firmly packed light brown sugar

1/2 cup granulated sugar

1 tsp vanilla

2 eggs

2 cups old-fashioned rolled oats

1 pkg (12 oz) semi-sweet chocolate chips

Preheat oven to 350°F. Grease baking sheets.

Combine flour, salt and baking soda.

Beat together shortening, sugars and vanilla in a large bowl until creamy. Add eggs, beating until light and fluffy. Gradually beat in flour mixture and rolled oats. Stir in chocolate chips.

Drop batter by well-rounded teaspoons onto greased baking sheets. Bake 8 to 10 minutes, or until golden.

Cool cookies on sheets on wire rack for 2 minutes. Remove cookies to wire rack to cool completely.

WOMEN *to* WOMEN
A Gift of Hope

Chocolate Chewies

1-1/2 cups unsalted
  butter

4 squares (4 oz)
  unsweetened chocolate

2-1/2 cups sugar,
  divided

3 eggs

1-1/2 tsp vanilla

2 cups flour

2 tsp baking powder

1/2 tsp salt

Cream butter in a bowl. Melt chocolate in a double boiler. Blend chocolate into butter with 2 cups of the sugar. Beat in eggs, one at a time. Add vanilla.

Sift flour, baking powder and salt together. Add to chocolate mixture.

Chill dough for 2 hours, then form dough into balls and roll in remaining sugar.

Place 2 inches apart on ungreased cookie sheet and bake 10 to 12 minutes at 350°F. Check at 10 minutes. *Do not overbake.* Should be chewy.

Makes about 50 cookies.

Vicki Lawrence Schultz

Actress and singer
Beverly Hills (and the beach),
California, U.S.A.

Gumdrop Cookies

1/2 cup butter

1/2 cup granulated
  sugar

1/2 cup brown sugar

1 egg

1/2 tsp vanilla

1 cup flour

1/2 tsp baking powder

1/2 tsp baking soda

pinch salt

1 cup rolled oats

1 cup gumdrops

Mix and spoon off in cookie-sized servings onto greased cookie sheets.

Bake at 350°F for 12 minutes.

Perhaps because she belongs to such a big family, Heather sent two recipes, and we decided to include both.–Editor

Sugar Ginger Cookies

1-1/2 cups granulated
  sugar

1 cup shortening

2 eggs

3/4 cup molasses

3 tsp baking soda

2 tsp baking powder

1 tsp salt

2 tsp ginger

1 tsp each cinnamon,
  nutmeg, cloves,
  allspice

3-1/2 cups flour

Cream together shortening and sugar. Add eggs and beat well. Stir in molasses.

Combine all dry ingredients and stir into the wet mixture. Roll into small balls, dip in sugar and place on greased cookie sheet. Don't flatten.

Bake at 350°F for 10 to 15 minutes.

Caroline Greyshock/95

Heather Rankin

*Singer / Member of
The Rankin Family*
Halifax, Nova Scotia, Canada

57

Bonnie Blair's Peanut Butter Cookies

"Skippy® Peanut Butter makes it special."

Rick Stewart/Allsport

1 cup butter

1 cup Skippy® Peanut Butter

1/2 tsp salt

1 cup granulated sugar

1 cup brown sugar, firmly packed

2 eggs, well beaten

1 tbsp milk

2 cups flour, sifted

1/2 tsp baking soda

Combine butter, peanut butter and salt. Mix well, gradually adding granulated sugar and brown sugar. Cream fairly well after each addition.

Add eggs and milk and mix well.

Sift flour and soda together and add to wet mixture.

Drop by teaspoonfuls on a greased cookie sheet. Flatten with a fork. Bake at 325°F for 15 to 20 minutes.

Bonnie Blair

Five-time Olympic speedskating champion
Milwaukee, Wisconsin, U.S.A.

WOMEN *to* WOMEN
A Gift of Hope

Chocolate-Dipped Strawberries

4 cups fresh strawberries   1 tbsp butter
6 oz semi-sweet chocolate   2 tsp brandy or liqueur

Wash strawberries, but do not hull. Place on paper towels to dry.

In a double boiler, melt chocolate. Stir in butter and brandy. Cool slightly. Dip pointed ends of strawberries into chocolate. Place on waxed paper to set.

Serve within 8 hours.

Makes about 4 servings.

Chocolate-Dipped Strawberries are pictured on page 159.

Sandie Rinaldo

CTV Television Network News Weekend Anchor, and Producer/Reporter/Writer for CTV's "Portrait" series
Toronto, Ontario, Canada

"I wish you good luck with this project. We will be watching for it."

Monda Rosenberg

Food Editor of Chatelaine
magazine, writer and
cookbook author
North York, Ontario, Canada

Homemade Lemon Squares

1 cup all-purpose flour	2 eggs
1/2 cup butter, at room temperature	2 tbsp freshly squeezed lemon juice
1/4 cup sifted icing sugar	1/4 cup shredded coconut, preferably unsweetened
1 cup granulated sugar	icing sugar
1/2 tsp baking powder	
1/4 tsp salt	

Preheat oven to 350°F. Butter an 8-inch-square baking pan. In a small bowl, stir flour with butter and icing sugar, using a spoon or a fork. Firmly press mixture into prepared baking pan, building up 1/2-inch sides.

Bake crust in centre of preheated oven until set and golden around edges, about 20 minutes. Remove from oven and set aside. Leave oven at 350°F.

In a small bowl, blend granulated sugar with baking powder and salt, using a fork. Beat in eggs, then add lemon juice. Beat mixture vigorously with fork until fluffy, about 3 minutes. Stir in coconut. Pour filling over crust.

Bake squares in centre of preheated oven until evenly browned and set, about 20 to 25 minutes. Cool in pan, then cut into squares and dust with icing sugar, if you wish.

Makes 16 squares.

WOMEN *to* WOMEN
A Gift of Hope

Quick and Easy Banana Bread

"This is a guaranteed 'no-fail' recipe! Wrapped tightly, it will keep in the fridge for several days."

1 cup granulated sugar

1/2 cup light oil

2 eggs

2 large ripe bananas, mashed

1/4 cup walnuts (optional)

1-1/4 cups flour

1 tsp baking soda

1 tsp baking powder

Combine sugar, oil, eggs, bananas and walnuts (if used) in a large bowl.

Sift together flour, baking soda and baking powder. Add to the wet mixture.

Pour into a greased and floured loaf pan. Bake 1 hour at 350°F.

Cool on a rack.

Roman Tarnavetsky

Lorraine Monk, OC

Author
Toronto, Ontario, Canada

"I am delighted to share this recipe, given to me by my best friend, Nancy Paul, Founder and first President of the Canadian Breast Cancer Foundation."

WOMEN *to* WOMEN
A Gift of Hope

You may have to fight a battle more than once to win it.

Margaret Thatcher

*The world is round and the place which
may seem like the end may also be
only the beginning.*

Ivy Baker Priest

Highlights

Savory and spicy accompaniments

Mona's Dip

1 cup sour cream
(regular or low-fat)

1 cup Hellmann's
mayonnaise
(or low-fat)

1/2 tsp garlic salt

1/2 tsp dill weed

1 tsp ground onion

1 tsp parsley

1 tsp beaumonde (made
by Island Spice
Company)

2 drops Tabasco sauce

Blend all together.

George Whiteside

Anne Murray

Recording artist
Toronto, Ontario, Canada

WOMEN *to* WOMEN
A Gift of Hope

Antipasto

"This a great recipe to make with a friend. Do all of the chopping first – takes about 2 hours. Don't use a blender!"

8 oz olive oil

1 very large head cauliflower, cut into bite-sized pieces

2 cans (14 oz each) ripe olives, chopped

1 can (16 oz) broken green olives, chopped

2 jars (12 oz each) pickled onions, chopped

2 cans (10 oz each) mushroom stems and pieces

2 large green peppers, chopped

2 cans (4 oz each) pimento, chopped

4 bottles (15 oz each) Heinz ketchup

1 bottle (15 oz) Heinz "hot" ketchup

1 jar (48 oz) mixed pickles, chopped

2 cans (1.8 oz each) anchovies, chopped (optional)

3 cans (7 oz each) solid tuna, chopped

3 cans (4 oz each) small shrimp

Michael Bedford Photography

Hon. Anne C. Cools

Liberal Senator,
Senate of Canada
Toronto, Ontario, Canada

Cook the oil, cauliflower, olives and onions for 10 minutes, stirring constantly. Add the mushrooms, green peppers, pimento, ketchup and mixed pickles. Simmer 10 minutes and stir often.

Drain the anchovies (if used), tuna and shrimp. Rinse with boiling water. Add to the simmering mixture. Spoon into sterilized jars, seal and process by placing jars on a rack in a large pot and adding 3 inches of water. Bring to a boil and simmer for 30 minutes. Keep in a cool place.

WOMEN to WOMEN
A Gift of Hope

Michael Bedford Photography

Hon. Joyce Fairbairn

Senator, Leader of the Government in the Senate, and Minister with Special Responsibility for Literacy
Lethbridge, Alberta, Canada

"Best wishes to your team. I applaud your efforts towards breast cancer research."

Green Tomato Mustard Relish

6 lbs (20) green tomatoes	1-1/2 cups flour
2-1/2 lbs (10) green peppers	1-1/2 tbsp salt
4 red peppers	1-1/2 tbsp turmeric
1-1/2 lbs (9) onions	1/2 cup prepared yellow mustard
4-1/2 cups sugar	4-1/2 cups white vinegar

Clean vegetables thoroughly. Put through medium grind in a food chopper. Drain.

Combine sugar, flour, salt, turmeric and mustard. Add vinegar slowly, stirring constantly to make a smooth blend. Add vegetables and boil gently until thick. Pour boiling mixture into hot, sterile jars. Seal immediately.

WOMEN to WOMEN
A Gift of Hope

Haricots verts à tarragon vinaigrette

Haricots

1 lb fresh green beans

Vinaigrette

1 tbsp red wine vinegar

3 tbsp good olive oil

1 tbsp mayonnaise

1 clove garlic, crushed

1/4 tsp tarragon

1/4 tsp dry mustard

1 tsp sea salt

lots of freshly ground
black pepper

2 tbsp chopped fresh
parsley

Trim, steam and cool the beans.

Mix the vinaigrette ingredients, then toss with
the beans.

*Haricots verts à tarragon vinaigrette are pictured
on page 36.*

Dini Petty

National talk-show host
Toronto, Ontario, Canada

Skordalia

"It's easy and wonderful for a large, informal gathering."

Beans

2 cups gigandes beans OR white limas

1 tsp salt

1/2 cup extra virgin olive oil

salt and freshly ground white pepper to taste

Skordalia

1 small potato

6 - 12 cloves garlic

6 slices Italian bread, crusts removed

warm water to soak

1 cup almonds, blanched OR pine nuts OR walnuts

2/3 cup good olive oil

juice of 1 fat lemon

salt and freshly ground white pepper to taste

Tabasco sauce (optional)

parsley for garnish

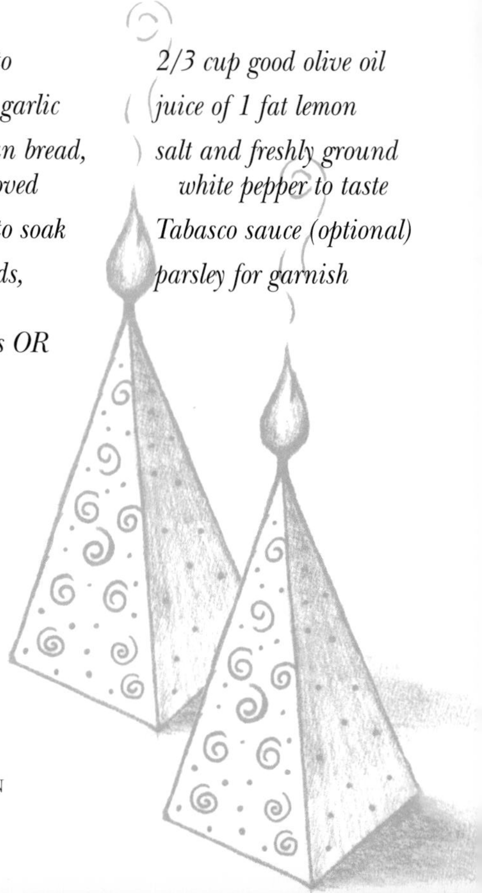

Sort the beans. Rinse, cover with water, and let soak overnight. Next day, rinse again, then pour into a heavy kettle and add fresh water to cover. Add 1 tsp of salt and bring to a boil. Cover, lower the heat, and let the beans simmer until just tender, about 90 minutes, give or take 15. Drain completely and put in a large bowl. Pour in 1/2 cup of olive oil, and season with salt and freshly ground white pepper. Let sit while you make the skordalia.

Peel the potato and boil until soft. Meantime, peel 6 to 12 cloves of garlic (the brave use an entire head). Cut 6 slices of Italian bread, throw away the crust, and soak the centres in warm water.

Mash the potato and put it into a food processor along with the blanched almonds and as many garlic cloves as you dare. Squeeze the bread dry and add to the bowl. Process until fairly smooth. With the motor running, drizzle in the olive oil, and purée until the sauce has the consistency of mayonnaise.

Blend in the juice of 1 fat lemon, and season with salt and freshly ground white pepper. Taste, adding more minced garlic or lemon, if you like, and a couple of shots of Tabasco.

To indulge, toss the beans in their oil, drain, and place on a platter. Sprinkle on a bit of parsley and spoon the skordalia into a mound alongside.

Pass the forks.

To eat them, you don't just scoop up a spoonful. You take a single bean on a fork and slide it through the sauce to get a good coating.

Pamela Wallin

Producer, journalist and broadcaster
Toronto, Ontario, Canada

"I am pleased to be part of a project where women can help other women."

69

Turnip Puff

6 cups 1-inch turnip
    cubes

2 tbsp butter

2 eggs, beaten

3 tbsp flour

1 tbsp brown sugar

1 tsp baking powder

3/4 tsp salt

1/8 tsp pepper

pinch nutmeg

1/2 cup fine dry bread
    crumbs

2 tbsp melted butter

Heat oven to 375°F. Butter a 1-1/2-quart casserole.

Cook turnip in boiling, salted water until tender. Drain and mash (should have about 3 cups). Add butter and eggs and beat well with a wooden spoon.

Combine flour, brown sugar, baking powder, salt, pepper and nutmeg. Then stir into the turnip mixture and spoon into prepared casserole.

Combine bread crumbs and melted butter and sprinkle over turnip.

Bake 25 minutes or until very hot, puffed, and lightly browned on top.

Turnip Puff is pictured on page 36.

Dr. Sylvia Fedoruk,

OC, SOM, MA, DSc, LLD, DHuML, FCCPM

*Retired
Former Lieutenant Governor
of Saskatchewan, Professor
Emeritus and former
Chancellor of the University of
Saskatchewan, Research
Scientist, and retired Medical
Radiation Physicist*
Saskatoon, Saskatchewan, Canada

WOMEN *to* WOMEN
A Gift of Hope

Spicy Sausage Rolls

"It's easy to make, freezes well, and they are wonderful for a party or lunch box."

1 lb top-quality lean
  sausage meat

1 tbsp ketchup

1-1/2 tsp HP Sauce

1/2 tsp celery seed

1/2 tsp garlic salt

1/2 tsp onion powder

1 tsp seasoning salt

1/2 tsp thyme

pepper to taste

1 pkg frozen puff pastry

Combine all ingredients except the pastry.

Roll the pastry as thin as possible. Cut into 7-inch squares. Put a strip of meat mixture at one end of the pastry and roll it up. Seal the ends, slash the top and brush with milk.

Bake at 375°F for about 20 to 25 minutes.

Makes 16 sausage rolls, each about 7 inches long.

Dr. Mary-Wynne Ashford

Physician and educator
Victoria, British Columbia, Canada

"This recipe is in remembrance of my dear friend Dr. Betty South, who died of breast cancer at 42."

Greek Spinach-Feta Casserole

"This dish is a favourite because with my hectic schedule and four hungry children to feed, time and nutrition are very important to me. If you cook the rice ahead of time, this is a very fast meal. Even my children, who hate cooked spinach, enjoy its taste when baked."

4 cups brown rice, cooked*

1 small onion, chopped fine

1 medium red pepper, chopped fine

1 small yellow pepper, chopped fine

4 cloves garlic, minced

5 eggs, beaten

1 cup skim milk

1-1/2 cups crumbled feta cheese

1/2 can or jar pitted calamata olives (optional)

3 tbsp tamari or soy sauce

1 tbsp crushed fennel seeds

1/2 cup chopped parsley

2 lbs (or 1 large bag) raw spinach, chopped

1-1/2 cups grated cheese to cover top of casserole

*3 cups brown rice and 1 cup wild rice can be mixed for a festive touch and increased nutritional value.

WOMEN *to* WOMEN
A Gift of Hope

Mix all ingredients together, in order, except the grated cheese. Spread into large buttered casserole and sprinkle top with grated cheese.

Bake for 45 to 60 minutes at 375°F until bubbling hot, and cheese is golden. Serve with Greek salad, pita and homous dip, for a Greek treat.

Serves 6 (large servings).

Lorna Vander Haeghe

Managing Editor of
The Healthy Living Guide, *owner of a nutritional supplement company, and freelance writer*
Burnaby, British Columbia, Canada

"I am the mother of four teenagers, all raised vegetarian."

Parsley and Rice Casserole

"A textured, nutty accompaniment to just about any meal. As I do tend to enjoy rich foods, it's great to find a recipe that I love which is healthy, too."

2 cups cooked wild rice

2 cups cooked white rice

4 cups cooked brown rice

2 tbsp natural oil

1 small or medium onion, chopped small

2 - 3 cloves garlic, minced

1 - 2 cups sliced mushrooms (optional)

1/2 cup pine nuts (optional)

2 cubes vegetable bouillon

1/2 cup water

1/4 - 1/2 cup nuts, ground

2 tbsp arrowroot powder

1 - 1-1/2 cups finely chopped fresh parsley

1 tsp dill weed

1 tsp sea salt

1 tsp paprika

WOMEN to WOMEN
A Gift of Hope

Cook rices separately, according to package directions. While the rice is cooking, sauté onions and garlic in hot oil until almost tender. Add mushrooms and pine nuts (if used), and sauté 1 to 2 minutes longer.

Preheat the oven to 350°F. Mix the hot rice with the bouillon cubes to soften them, and combine thoroughly. Add the sautéed mixture and all of the remaining ingredients to the rice, and mix carefully so as to not mash the rice.

Place the mixture in a lightly oiled, deep 9-inch or 10-inch baking dish, and smooth the top. Sprinkle on extra paprika for added appeal. Bake for about 30 minutes until hot and somewhat firm throughout. Serve immediately.

Keeps refrigerated for 5 to 7 days. Best if not frozen.

Patricia Patkau

Architect and Associate Professor, University of British Columbia
Vancouver, British Columbia, Canada

Baked Eggplant Casserole
("Sheik el Mihshee" in Arabic)

"A well-known Middle East recipe as taught me by my mother. This is one of my favourite recipes because it is Middle Eastern (my heritage), and because it is nutritious, light and yummy."

2 large (or 3 medium) eggplants

1-1/2 lbs lean lamb or beef, minced

1 onion, chopped

1/2 cup pine nuts

dash each allspice, nutmeg, cinnamon

1-1/2 tsp salt (total)

1/4 tsp pepper

1 can (8 oz) tomato sauce

2 tbsp lemon juice

1/2 cup hot water

WOMEN to WOMEN
A Gift of Hope

Peel and slice eggplants in 1/2-inch slices. Sprinkle with about 1 tsp of salt, and let stand for about 1 hour or more to remove the excess moisture. Blot eggplant slices.

Place sliced eggplants under the broiler and brown lightly on each side. (May be brushed with melted butter prior to broiling.)

Sauté meat and onions until meat is cooked.

Sauté pine nuts slightly on very low heat in a non-stick frying pan. Add pine nuts to meat mixture, with 1/2 tsp salt, pepper and spices.

Arrange slices of eggplant on the bottom of a 9-inch by 13-inch baking pan. (I prefer Pyrex.) Spread meat mixture over slices of eggplant and cover with remaining eggplant slices.

Mix tomato sauce, lemon juice and hot water, and pour over the casserole.

Bake in a 375°F oven for 40 minutes until the eggplant is well cooked but still firm.

Usually served with rice.

©Jon Joosten Photography

Dr. Helen K. Mussallem, CC

Special advisor to national and international health organizations
Ottawa, Ontario, Canada

Mary Kay's Jalapeño Dressing (For Turkey)

2 cups yellow cornmeal

2 cups all-purpose flour, sifted

1/3 cup sugar

8 tsp baking powder

1 tsp salt

2 eggs

2 cups milk

1/2 cup soft shortening

1/4 - 1/2 cup bacon drippings

1 bunch green onions, chopped

1/2 stalk celery, including leaves, chopped

1 cup water

3 cups cornbread, crumbled

4 cups day-old bread

2 or 3 cups (or more) turkey broth

1 cup (yes, 1 cup!) jalapeño juice

salt and pepper to taste

chopped jalapeños, to taste

Preheat oven to 425°F.

Sift together cornmeal, flour, sugar, baking powder and salt into a bowl. Add eggs, milk and shortening. Beat with rotary beater until smooth, about 1 minute.

Bake in 2, 8-inch square baking pans in a hot (preheated) oven for 20 to 25 minutes.

Sauté onions and celery in bacon drippings. Add water, cover, and cook until barely tender, about 7 minutes. Combine with the last 6 ingredients. Add water until it's the right consistency, if necessary.

Stuff turkey with dressing. Place excess dressing in a greased casserole and bake at 350°F for 30 minutes.

Mary Kay Ash

Founder and Chair Emeritus of Mary Kay Cosmetics
Dallas, Texas, U.S.A.

"I wish you tremendous success. Someday soon our hopes will be realized, and the battle will be won, and breast cancer will be beaten."

The Common and Elegant Baked Potato

Source: "Legendary. Baked potatoes are the ultimate comfort food, and excellent for one's health."

It used to be that potatoes were the bad guys in our diet, full of unnecessary calories, without precious protein, mere starch for the stodgy at heart. So it was with pleasure that I learned, eventually, that potatoes are full of vitamins and fibre and not quite the calorie-carriers that we once thought – only about a hundred, in fact.

Microwaved "baked potatoes" don't do it for me. I like to preheat a good hot oven to about 375 degrees, and put my scrubbed and punctured and buttered potatoes in for about an hour. I turn them over once if I think about it. You can also put them in for two hours at 250 degrees, for the potato is a forgiving vegetable. It wants to please.

WOMEN to WOMEN
A Gift of Hope

Baked potatoes go with everything, and can even be served on their own. Portions are no problem. Simply bake one potato per person; what could be easier?

I do slit them before serving, just to keep them from skittering around on the plate, and with them we provide at our house a dish of low-fat yogurt in which I've chopped a green onion or two, or perhaps a few leaves of cilantro. Of course we eat the skins too, and consider them the best part.

Carol Shields

Novelist
Winnipeg, Manitoba, Canada

"I love to eat, therefore I cook."

Great, Low-Fat, Delicious, Almost-Roasted Potatoes

Make sure you use baking potatoes, but don't peel the skin. Score lightly.

Cut in half.

Pour 1 tbsp of olive oil on a baking sheet. Add a little salt and pepper. You can also add any other seasoning you prefer. I enjoy Cajun seasoning.

Rub the flesh part of the potato in the oil and seasoning, and leave the flesh side down on the sheet.

Bake for 45 minutes at 425°F.

Enjoy.

Great, Low-Fat, Delicious, Almost-Roasted Potatoes are pictured on page 36.

Valerie Pringle

Television Co-host of CTV Television Network's
Canada AM
Toronto, Ontario, Canada

"No one is immune or untouched. As women, we must do everything we can to prevent breast cancer, protect each other, and promote the issue. This is in memory and in hope."

WOMEN *to* WOMEN
A Gift of Hope

Yukon "Chilly" Sauce

"With my work, I don't always have time to spend preparing elaborate meals. This recipe came from a friend, and is a tasty sauce that turns a simple meal into something special."

20 ripe tomatoes, peeled and diced

2 cups granulated sugar

2 cups white vinegar

2 tbsp coarse pickling salt

6 medium onions, finely chopped

1 sweet red pepper

1 small hot pepper (optional)

2 tbsp mixed whole spices in a cheesecloth bag

Mix all ingredients together and bring to a boil. Let simmer for two hours, stirring occasionally.

Prepare for canning, and voilà! Yukon "chilly" sauce!

(Especially delicious with pasta and cheese.)

Hon. Audrey McLaughlin, MP

Member of Parliament, Yukon
Whitehorse, Yukon, Canada

"As a Member of the Canadian Parliament, Women's Critic for the New Democratic Party, and as a woman, I am pleased to be a part of Celebrity Lights and to help in the fight against breast cancer. This project reminds me of what anthropologist Margaret Mead once said: 'Never doubt that a small group of thoughtful, committed citizens can change the world; indeed, it's the only thing that ever has'."

WOMEN *to* WOMEN
A Gift of Hope

I wanted a perfect ending.
Now I've learned, the hard way, that some poems
don't rhyme, and some stories
don't have a clear beginning, middle, and end.
Life is about not knowing,
having to change, taking the moment and
making the best of it,
without knowing what's going to happen next.

Gilda Radner

All things are possible until they are proved impossible -
and even the impossible may only be so, as of now.

Pearl S. Buck

Twilight

Light supper dishes for twilit evenings

Chinese Poached Chicken in a Garden by Summer Twilight

"This is a family recipe. I like it because it always works, and it makes the best poached chicken – not only for this particular recipe, but also for any other poached chicken dish. It is a centuries-old method that produces chicken which is juicy and cooked right through to the bone, but never dry."

3 - 4 lb very good quality, free-range chicken

5 - 6 green onions

1 bunch coriander, chopped

2 walnut-shaped knobs of ginger, peeled

2 tbsp dark soy sauce

2 tsp sugar

1 - 2 tbsp peanut oil

some sesame oil

Try to use the heavy, French kind of enamelled casserole that will just hold the chicken and the liquid to cover it.

Place the chicken in the casserole with room-temperature water, just to cover. Bring to a boil and quickly lower to simmer. Simmer, uncovered, for exactly 20 minutes. Put the lid on the casserole and turn off the heat. Leave the

WOMEN *to* WOMEN
A Gift of Hope

chicken in the covered casserole until the whole thing comes to room temperature. (This will take anywhere from 4 to 6 hours, depending on the temperature of your room.)

Take the chicken out and drain it. Reserve the liquid for other uses. Put some sesame oil on your hands and rub it all over the chicken. (The reserved liquid can be boiled down to make a couple of cups of good broth, or added to other things you're cooking at the same time.)

Slice the chicken off the bones in nice, neat pieces and lay them in one layer on a pretty, oval serving plate. I like to reconstruct the form of the chicken on the plate, with the wings at the top and the legs at the bottom. Be sure to keep the skin on. That is part of the Chinese flavour.

Chop the green onions into 2-inch lengths, and then into strips. Cut up the ginger into little sticks. In a heavy frying pan, combine the oil, soy sauce, sugar, green onion and ginger. Heat just to boiling, until the sugar is dissolved. Pour over the chicken, distributing evenly. Leave for an hour or so before eating. Sprinkle with lots of chopped coriander just before serving.

Serve with steamed rice and a stir-fried vegetable like bok choy, Chinese mustard greens, or, if you are desperate, broccoli.

Chinese Poached Chicken in a Garden by Summer Twilight is pictured on page 101.

Adrienne Clarkson

Broadcaster and Chair, Board of Trustees, Canadian Museum of Civilization
Toronto, Ontario, Canada

"Cooking is a wonderful thing to do. I lose myself in it completely!"

Chinese Beef with Crisp Vegetables

"Quick, nutritious, and tastes like you spent hours. Can be light, with chicken, or rich, with fillet of beef."

Vegetables

1 tbsp vegetable oil

2 tsp crushed garlic

8 oz lean beef, thinly sliced

1-1/2 cups chopped broccoli

1-1/2 cups thinly sliced sweet red pepper

1-1/2 cups snow peas

Sauce

1 tbsp cornstarch

3/4 cup beef stock

2 tbsp soy sauce

1/4 cup brown sugar

2 tbsp sherry or rice vinegar

1-1/2 tsp minced ginger root OR 1/4 tsp ground ginger

WOMEN *to* WOMEN
A Gift of Hope

In a small bowl, combine sauce ingredients. Mix well and set aside.

In a large non-stick skillet, heat oil. Sauté garlic and beef just until the beef is browned but not cooked through. Remove beef and set aside.

To the skillet, add broccoli, red pepper and snow peas; sauté for 2 minutes. Return beef to the pan. Stir sauce and add to the pan. Cook, stirring constantly, just until beef is cooked and sauce has thickened, approximately 2 minutes.

Serves 4.

Make ahead

Prepare sauce early in the day, and use as a marinade for the beef. Refrigerate. Drain before cooking, and use sauce as indicated.

Judith Maxwell

Economist and Policy Analyst
Ottawa, Ontario, Canada

"We must all try to create hope for those who need it."

Wei's Noodle Salad

"My own creation. I don't use recipes or measure … my cooking is free flowing, so please adjust quantities at leisure."

Salad

cooked noodles for 4
(spaghetti, Chinese
noodles or vermicelli)

1 red pepper, cut into
small strips

1 yellow pepper, cut into
small strips

1/2 English cucumber,
cut into strips

1 large carrot, grated

1/4 cup chopped
cilantro

1/4 cup chopped fresh
basil

1/4 cup chopped green
onions

Dressing

Adjust liquids to taste
and combine to make
about 1/2 cup:

soy sauce
fish sauce
hoisin sauce
rice wine vinegar
sesame oil

1 tsp crushed fresh
ginger

WOMEN to WOMEN
A Gift of Hope

Prepare vegetables while noodles cook.

Whisk together dressing as you would a vinaigrette, or shake in a jar.

Let noodles cool a bit, so as not to cook the vegetables.

Simply toss everything together and serve warm or cold. It can be prepared ahead of time.

Substitutions

What I love about this recipe is its simplicity and versatility. You can add chicken or shrimp, freshly cooked or recycled leftovers. Sometimes I use roasted peppers, and sometimes I stir-fry everything except the cucumber.

To get a Thai flavour, you can add chopped egg omelet and chopped peanuts on top, and some coconut milk to the dressing. Or you could omit the basil, put some wasabi in the dressing, and sprinkle the salad with nori and sesame seeds.

That's the best part – you can modify this recipe any way you wish. You can serve it as a light main course, or a side dish, or take it to a potluck. I find it a very popular salad option during barbecue season. I have given this recipe to many people who have enjoyed it. Hope you do, too.

Wei Chen

Television News Anchor
Toronto, Ontario, Canada

"Hope is like a beacon. Without it, we would be lost in the darkness of despair. Good luck with the book. May it bring light to the lives of many."

Wei's Noodle Salad is pictured on page 102.

Pork Chow Mein

"My Mom invented and perfected this recipe over the years. It's easy to make in large quantities, it freezes well, it microwaves well to reheat, and it tastes great!"

2 boneless butterfly pork chops

12 cups water

4 bags steam-fried noodles

1 large onion, coarsely chopped

2 - 3 stalks celery, finely sliced on diagonal

1 head sui choy (or napa cabbage), coarsely chopped

2 handfuls bean sprouts, rinsed

garlic powder to taste

2 - 3 tbsp vegetable oil

China Lily soy sauce

toasted sesame seeds (optional)

WOMEN *to* WOMEN
A Gift of Hope

Trim all fat off pork. Cube. Sprinkle liberally with garlic powder. Add pork to about 12 cups of water, bring to a boil, reduce heat and simmer 1-1/2 to 2 hours. Remove pork and reserve broth.

Heat oil in stock pot, add pork to brown over medium heat. When pork is browned, add celery and cook 1 to 2 minutes, then add sui choy and onion. Sauté until the vegetables are tender. Add sprouts and reduce heat to low.

Add noodles, 1/2 a bag at a time. Also begin adding just enough stock to moisten. Add broth slowly ... too much makes chow mein soggy. Also alternately sprinkle the mixture with soy sauce during this mixing stage. Add enough to darken the mixture slightly.

When all noodles are added and just moistened, cover pot and allow to steam at least 1 hour (2 hours is better). Stir often to avoid sticking or burning.

Serve sprinkled with toasted sesame seeds (optional). Serve with rice, or any Chinese dish.

Leftovers can be frozen, and reheated in the microwave on high for about 2 minutes per serving.

Lisa Walters

Professional golfer on the LPGA Tour
Tampa, Florida, U.S.A.

"When I have to cook ... STAY OUT OF MY KITCHEN!!"

Dilled Orange and Almond Chicken Stir-Fry

"The flavour is superb, and it's so easy to make."

1 lb skinless, boneless chicken breast halves

2 carrots

3/4 cup broccoli flowerets

3/4 cup sliced zucchini

3/4 cup snow peas

3/4 cup diced onion

1/2 cup diced celery

1/2 cup sliced red pepper

grated rind from 1 orange

1 tsp salt

1/2 tsp pepper

2 tsp dried dill weed

1/2 tsp dried thyme

3/4 cup fresh orange juice (frozen may be substituted)

1 cup chicken broth

2 tsp cornstarch

1/4 cup water

1 can (10 oz) mandarin oranges

1/4 cup slivered almonds

2 cups cooked rotini

WOMEN to WOMEN
A Gift of Hope

Cut vegetables and set aside. Cut chicken into thin strips. Heat a large non-stick pan over medium heat. Stir-fry chicken until just cooked, about 7 minutes. Add vegetables and continue to cook for about another 4 minutes. Add seasonings, juice and chicken broth. Bring to a boil.

In a small bowl mix cornstarch and water. Once sauce is bubbling, gradually add the cornstarch and water to slightly thicken the sauce, using only as much of the cornstarch mixture as needed. Reduce the heat to low and continue to cook for about 2 minutes.

Serve over rotini and sprinkle with orange sections and a few almonds.

Serves 5.

Variations

Substitute cooked rice or bulgur for the rotini.

Marg Ruttan

Cookbook author and magazine publisher
Calgary, Alberta, Canada

"Thank you for the opportunity to contribute to such a worthwhile project. I had so many blessings in my life and it isn't often that there's a chance to give something back in such a meaningful way, but this project certainly provides that opportunity. What a great way to empower women!"

Warm Lentil Salad

"You can prepare this ahead of time, but it tastes best warm. Freshly made, it elevates the humble lentil to culinary heights it never dreamed of."

2 cups green lentils

4 cups cold water

1 onion, halved, each
half stuck with 2 cloves

1/2 tsp salt

1 bay leaf

1 onion

3/8 cup extra virgin
olive oil

1 tbsp salt

juice of 1 lemon

black pepper to taste

1/2 cup finely chopped
parsley

1 clove garlic, pressed

2 tbsp finely chopped
fresh mint (optional)

WOMEN to WOMEN
A Gift of Hope

Put lentils in a pot with the water, the onion stuck with cloves, the 1/2 tsp salt, and the bay leaf. Bring to a boil. Reduce heat, cover and simmer for 40 minutes.

Right after you put lentils on to cook, peel the other onion, cut it in half, slice it thinly and put it in a large bowl with the olive oil and the 1 tbsp of salt. Mix well and set aside. (The reason for this is that the salt causes the onion to give up its juice, which has two tasty results: the oil takes on a wonderful onion-juice flavour, and the onion mellows sweetly.)

When the lentils are cooked, drain them and discard the onion halves with cloves.

Add the warm lentils to the bowl with the onions and oil. Add the lemon juice and a few grindings of black pepper, along with the parsley, garlic and optional mint.

Serves 6.

Joanne Kates

Director of Camp Arowhon in Algonquin Park, and Restaurant Critic for The Globe and Mail
Toronto, Ontario, Canada

"All the best with the project. We need it!"

Pasta Primavera

"This is my favourite recipe because it is nourishing, tasty and healthy."

Choose whole wheat pasta, as it contains fibre, and serve it with a light tomato-and-herb sauce. Do not be tempted into topping it with a rich or cream sauce high in calories.

2 cups (18 oz) penne	8 large mushrooms
1 head broccoli	2 large tomatoes
2 medium courgettes (zucchini)	2 cloves garlic
2 medium onions	grated parmesan cheese (optional)

Cook pasta in boiling water for 12 minutes (until *al dente*). Drain and refresh with boiling water (to remove excess starch).

Break broccoli head into flowerets and cook in a steamer or colander over boiling water. Steam for 7 minutes approximately (so broccoli is cooked, but still crunchy).

Chop onions coarsely and sauté in a little butter until soft. (If you have a microwave oven, no butter is needed. Put onions in a bowl with about 1/2 inch of water at the bottom. Cover with cling film and cook at high for 2-1/2 minutes. Drain when cooked.) Add onions to the steamed broccoli.

WOMEN *to* WOMEN
A Gift of Hope

Wash courgettes (zucchini) and cut into 2-inch strips. Cook in the steamer for about 5 minutes, or boil in water until cooked but not too soft.

Clean mushrooms with a little salt and paper towels, or peel them. Place under a hot grill for a few minutes. Drain on paper towels. When cooked, cut into large chunks.

Concasse tomatoes by placing them in boiling water for 10 seconds, then transfer them immediately to cold water. This allows you to remove the skin. Quarter, and cut each quarter in half again. Remove the seeds.

Crush garlic and add to vegetables. Season with salt and pepper. Add vegetables (except the broccoli) to the pasta and reheat gently in a saucepan.

Place broccoli back in the steamer for a minute to reheat, and then carefully add to the hot pasta and vegetables. This prevents the broccoli from breaking up. Add your favourite sauce.

Add a little grated parmesan for more flavour, but this is not essential. Serve warm – not too hot. It's scrumptious, and a healthy dish that children will savour.

Serves 4.

Gary Bernstein

Joan Collins

Actress and author
London, England

Pasta Primavera is pictured on page 103.

Nancy Marino

Producer of
The Second City
Toronto, Ontario, Canada

Light and Easy Primo Pasta Sauce

"This is my favourite recipe because it's light, quick to prepare and delicious ... full of flavour."

l large can whole plum tomatoes

3 - 4 cloves garlic, chopped or crushed

1 tbsp olive oil

1 tbsp capers

4 anchovy fillets, chopped

1/2 can whole black olives, sliced

1 tsp Italian seasoning

pinch crushed chili peppers

freshly grated parmesan cheese for garnish

Heat oil and sauté garlic briefly. Add remaining ingredients. Let simmer for 1 hour. Pour over your favourite pasta (rigatoni, penne, ravioli). Garnish with freshly grated parmesan cheese. Serve with a garden salad and Italian bread.

WOMEN *to* WOMEN
A Gift of Hope

Chinese Poached Chicken in a Garden by Summer Twilight,
from Adrienne Clarkson. See page 86.

Curry Rice Salad, left, from Gillian Anderson. See page 46.
Wei's Noodle Salad, right, from Wei Chen. See page 90.

Pasta Primavera, from Joan Collins. See page 98.

Diana Krall's West Coast Clams. See page 106.

104

Joy's Fabulous Fish Cakes

"Fish cakes are so easy to make and so wholesome. You can substitute any leftover fish that you have."

1 lb mature potatoes
(new potatoes won't
mash)

1 lb salmon, cooked and
flaked
OR 2 cans (7 oz each)
of salmon, drained

1 egg

1/2 cup finely chopped
onion

1/4 cup finely chopped
celery

1/4 cup finely chopped
green pepper
(optional)

light olive or canola oil

chopped parsley
for garnish (optional)

Joy Metcalfe

Broadcast journalist
Vancouver, British Columbia, Canada

"The fight against breast cancer is so worthy that I'm happy to be involved."

Boil potatoes, drain and mash. Add flaked fish to mashed potatoes. Stir in egg, onion, celery and green pepper (if used) until well mixed.

Shape into 8 fish cakes, each about 1/2 inch thick. Brown in light olive or canola oil and cook until golden brown. Sprinkle chopped parsley on top, if desired.

Serve with green salad, coleslaw or simple slices of tomatoes and cucumber.

WOMEN *to* WOMEN
A Gift of Hope

Diana Krall's West Coast Clams

"I often make this for my family, and I've enjoyed adding other ingredients ... plus our famous Nanaimo clams."

3 lbs fresh West Coast clams

1 or 2 cloves garlic, crushed

1 large shallot
OR 3 tbsp green onion, chopped

1/4 - 1/2 cup butter

1 can (14 oz) Italian tomatoes, undrained

1 cup dry white wine

1/2 cup canned clam nectar
OR water OR wine

salt and pepper to taste

any fresh (or pinch of dried) Italian herbs, such as basil

dash of hot crushed chili peppers (optional)

fresh parsley for garnish (optional)

WOMEN to WOMEN
A Gift of Hope

Scrub clams in several changes of cold water, or follow market directions.

Melt butter in a large, shallow pan. Sauté garlic and shallot or onion in butter. Cover and simmer gently for just a few minutes so as not to burn the garlic. Add the tomatoes, plus their juice, clam nectar, water or more wine, spices, salt and pepper.

Bring to a gentle boil, add clams and reduce heat to low so that the clams simmer until the shells open, about 6 to 8 minutes.

Discard any shells that don't open.

To serve, place several clams in each serving bowl and ladle the juice on top. Sprinkle with fresh parsley and serve with plenty of fresh bread to sop up the juices.

Variation

On my last trip home, I found this to be a nice variation of my first recipe:

Diana Krall's Clams with Tequila and Fresh Cilantro

Add 1/2 cup tequila in place of the wine, or in addition to the wine. Before serving, add fresh chopped cilantro in place of the parsley. Be sure to include hot or mild crushed chilies.

Diana Krall's West Coast Clams are pictured on page 104.

Diana Krall

Canadian jazz singer/pianist and recording artist
Nanaimo, British Columbia, Canada

"Living in New York is energizing, but I love to come home often to the West Coast and Vancouver Island, where I can be by the ocean, ski, and spend time with my family and friends."

107

Stephen's Fruits de Mer Provençale

"Tasty, elegant, simple to make, and makes me dream of Provence! As a soup for an alfresco light summer lunch, or as a first course for a dinner party, this is similar to a rich bouillabaisse, but uses no cream or fats. It makes an excellent first course and contrast to grilled veal chops or steaks.

"Almost all of the preparation and cooking can be done the day before or just before serving, so it is essentially a heat-and-serve dish.

"It is important to cut the fish into small enough bite-sized pieces. Cooking the soup base in the oven permits a controlled and hands-off preparation. Stovetop simmering also works well, but requires more care."

2 cups diced, peeled
   tomatoes (canned
   tomatoes work well)
2 large potatoes, peeled
   and sliced about
   1/8 inch thick
1 large onion, diced
3 leeks, diced
3 cups homemade
   chicken stock
3 cloves garlic, sliced
4 bay leaves

1/2 tsp thyme
vegetable oil to sauté
1-1/2 lbs fillet of fresh
   monkfish
1/2 lb small tiger
   prawns or large
   shrimp (fresh)
2 squid tubes (usually
   frozen: clean and
   wash immediately,
   then refrigerate in a
   covered container)
salt and pepper to taste
fresh chopped herbs, to
   taste

WOMEN to WOMEN
A Gift of Hope

Soup Base

Combine the tomatoes, potatoes, onion, garlic, chicken stock and spices in a large casserole. Simmer, uncovered, in a 300°F oven for 2 hours, or until onions and potatoes are cooked. Add the reserved leeks, and simmer for a further 15 minutes. Do not overcook the leeks. Cool and process in a blender until well chopped, but *do not liquefy*. Add salt and pepper to taste. Refrigerate.

Bring to the boil a large pot of salted water. Add shrimp/prawns. Cook for 2 minutes. Drain and quench the shrimp/prawns in cold water. Peel and refrigerate.

Fish Soup

(Prepare 15 to 20 minutes before serving.)

Reheat the soup base so that it comes to a simmer in about 10 minutes.

Slice squid into bite-sized rounds and sauté in very hot vegetable oil for 3 to 4 minutes. Slice cooked shrimp in half, lengthways. Set both aside.

Trim off tough membrane (a slight purplish colour on one side of the fillet) from monkfish, and discard. Slice fillet into bite-sized portions about 1/3 inch thick.

After the soup base has simmered for 5 minutes, increase the heat slightly and add the sliced monkfish. Cook for 5 minutes. Add the cooked shrimp and squid at the 3-minute point in order to reheat them, and serve directly.

Serve in soup bowls with a garnish of chopped fresh herbs such as parsley, basil or coriander for a different finishing taste, and thin rounds of toasted French bread, drizzled with virgin olive oil.

Serves 8.

Michael Dismatek Photography

Geraldine Kenney-Wallace

Scientist, professor and business woman
Toronto, Ontario, Canada

"Dedicated to Joan Kenney, my long-late mother, and Florence Cooper (formerly Wallace), my lively mother-in-law, this recipe reflects Stephen Wallace's heritage growing up on Vancouver Island. Cancer has been the major cause of death for generations of my family – breast cancer in particular. As scientists, Stephen and I believe that light and healthy cooking can help reduce risks, as medical research continues to identify the risk factors we all face, and the solutions."

109

My candle burns at both ends;
It will not last the night;
But, ah, my foes, and, oh, my friends -
It gives a lovely light.

Edna St. Vincent Millay

If you have knowledge,
let others light their candles in it.

Margaret Fuller

Candlelight

Full entrées and hearty dishes for dinner

WOMEN *to* WOMEN
A Gift of Hope

The Rt. Hon. Kim Campbell

Lawyer, North America's first female head of state, former Prime Minister of Canada and Defence Minister
Vancouver, British Columbia, Canada

South African Bobotie

1-1/2 lbs hamburger meat

1 cup bread crumbs or soft bread

2 eggs

1/2 cup milk

1/2 cup dried apricots cut into quarters

1 tsp salt

1 large onion

1 tbsp sugar

4 - 6 tsp curry powder (to taste)

3 tbsp water

Slice onion and sauté until tender but not too brown. Add sugar and curry, and stir. Add water. Cover and simmer for 5 minutes.

Combine meat, bread crumbs, salt and apricots in a large bowl.

Beat eggs with milk, and set aside.

Add onion mixture to the meat, and enough of the egg/milk mixture (about three-quarters) to achieve a meatloaf consistency.

Press into an 8-inch by 8-inch cake pan. Pour remaining egg/milk mixture over the top, and dot with butter. Bake at 375°F for 60 to 70 minutes.

Delicious hot or cold. If serving cold, drain and chill, and cut in slices one-third the pan width, by 1/2 an inch.

WOMEN *to* WOMEN
A Gift of Hope

Linguine Exotica

"I've always enjoyed trying different types of vegetables, such as eggplant, zucchini, etc. And since my favourite meal is pasta, I've learned to be creative and somewhat calorie-conscious at the same time."

1 tbsp butter
OR 1/2 cup oil

1/2 medium onion, chopped

8 large mushrooms, sliced

1/2 red pepper, julienned

1/2 small jar quartered artichoke hearts, in water

1/2 small eggplant, cubed

1 jar Classico pasta sauce

1 pkg linguine

feta cheese for garnish

1 bottle dry Chilean red wine

In a saucepan, heat the butter or oil. Sauté onion, mushrooms and red pepper on high. After 2 minutes, add the artichoke hearts. (Use the other 1/2 of the jar tomorrow in a salad.) Add the eggplant. You may need a little extra butter at this point.

After approximately 5 minutes, add 1 jar of your favourite Classico pasta sauce. Simmer for 5 to 7 minutes while you cook your linguine.

When the linguine appears tender, throw a piece against the wall to make sure it's ready (or just for the fun of it!).

You are ready to serve.

I like to sprinkle a little feta cheese on top, and serve with a bottle of dry Chilean red wine.

Bon appétit!

Patricia Conroy

Country music recording artist
Hendersonville, Tennessee, U.S.A.

"I rarely eat dessert, so I don't have a favourite dessert recipe – I'd rather eat more pasta!"

WOMEN *to* WOMEN
A Gift of Hope

Spinach Stuffed Manicotti

"I love pasta, and spinach is very good for you!"

Pasta

20 manicotti

4 qts boiling water

1 tbsp cooking oil
(optional)

1 tbsp salt

Stuffing

1 lb Italian sausage

2 eggs

2 cups grated mozzarella cheese

1 cup cottage cheese

1/2 cup grated parmesan cheese

1/4 cup dry bread crumbs

10 oz frozen chopped spinach, thawed

sprinkle salt

light sprinkle pepper

1/8 tsp nutmeg

1/8 tsp garlic powder

Tomato Sauce

2 cans (14 oz each) stewed tomatoes

1 cup chopped onions

1 bay leaf

1/2 tsp oregano

1/2 tsp basil

5-1/2 oz tomato paste

1/4 cup grated parmesan cheese

Cook manicotti in boiling water, cooking oil (if used) and salt in an uncovered Dutch oven until barely tender, about 5 to 6 minutes. Drain. Rinse with cold water.

Remove casings from sausages. Scramble-fry meat. Drain and set aside.

Beat eggs lightly in a bowl. Add next 9 ingredients. Add sausage meat. Mix together. Stuff manicotti. Set aside.

Combine all sauce ingredients except parmesan cheese in a saucepan. Bring to a boil. Simmer uncovered, stirring often, until sauce has boiled down and thickened, about 15 to 20 minutes. Discard bay leaf.

Use a baking pan that is large enough to hold the manicotti close together in a single layer. Spoon enough sauce into the bottom of the pan to cover. Place the manicotti on the sauce layer. Pour the remaining sauce over the manicotti. Bake uncovered in a 350°F oven for 20 minutes.

Sprinkle with parmesan cheese. Bake 10 more minutes.

Makes 20 manicotti / serves 2 or 3 people.

Spinach Stuffed Manicotti are pictured on page 121.

Sylvie Fréchette

Marketing Representative for the National Bank of Canada, and Olympic gold medallist in solo synchronized swimming
Montréal, Québec, Canada

"Life is not a having and a getting, but being and becoming."

Linguine with Tomatoes and Basil

John Hryniuk Photography

Hon.
Ethel Blondin-Andrew, MP

*Member of Parliament,
Secretary of State for Training
and Youth, and first (and still
only) aboriginal woman to sit
in the House of Commons
Yellowknife, Northwest Territories,
Canada*

*"I am more than happy to help in any
way in the fight against breast cancer.
I hope your unique endeavour is a
tremendous success, and I offer you
my best wishes."*

"It's my favourite recipe because it's a nutritious,
fast, hot meal, and everybody I've served it to
loved it."

*4 large ripe tomatoes, cut
into 1/2-inch cubes*

*1 lb Brie cheese, rind
removed, torn into
irregular pieces*

*1 cup fresh basil leaves,
cleaned and cut into
strips*

*3 cloves garlic, peeled
and finely minced*

*1 cup + 1 tbsp best-
quality olive oil*

2-1/2 tsp salt

*1/2 tsp freshly ground
black pepper*

*1-1/2 lbs linguine (fresh,
if you can get it)*

*freshly grated parmesan
cheese for garnish
(optional)*

Prepare at least 2 hours before serving and set
aside, covered, at room temperature. In a large
serving bowl, combine tomatoes, Brie, basil,
garlic, 1 cup of the olive oil, 1/2 tsp of the salt,
and pepper.

Bring 6 quarts of water to a boil in a large pot.
Add 1 tbsp olive oil and remaining salt. Add the
linguine and boil until tender but still firm, 8 to
10 minutes (only 3 to 5 minutes if it's fresh pasta).

Drain pasta and immediately toss with the tomato
sauce. Serve at once, passing
the pepper mill, and grated
parmesan cheese if you like.

Serves 4 to 6.

WOMEN *to* WOMEN
A Gift of Hope

Lasagna

Lasagna

16 oz lasagna (or very wide) noodles, cooked

2 or 3 pkgs mozzarella cheese, sliced

1 can parmesan cheese

Meat Sauce

2 lbs best ground beef, browned

2 cans (1 lb each) tomatoes

2 cans (8 oz each) tomato sauce

2 pkgs spaghetti sauce mix

garlic to taste (as much as you like)

Cook for 40 minutes, covered.

Cottage Cheese Mix

2 pints creamy cottage cheese

black pepper to taste

2 whole eggs

Mix well in a bowl.

Place in 2 casseroles (13 by 9 by 2 inches) in layers: noodles, mozzarella cheese, cottage cheese mix, meat sauce.

Meat sauce goes on top. Sprinkle top with grated parmesan cheese, and bake at 350°F for 30 minutes. Let stand 15 minutes before cutting in squares.

Can be made in advance and reheated. (Most of us use smaller casseroles or aluminum pans and freeze them, so we can be set at any time for unexpected company. All it needs is a favourite salad to rest beside on the plate.)

Serves 12.

Milne Photography

Pauline Hill

Honourary Chair, Welcome Wagon Ltd.
Agincourt, Ontario, Canada

Women to Women
A Gift of Hope

117

Sharon Hampson

*Children's entertainer
(Sharon, Lois & Bram)*
Toronto, Ontario, Canada

*"As a two-time breast cancer survivor,
I am delighted to participate in this
project."*

*Sharon's Enchilada Lasagna is
pictured on page 122.*

Sharon's Enchilada Lasagna

"Our favourite family meal is Mexican food, which
we have been eating for years. Currently, there are
four generations of us enjoying this dish."

2 cups sour cream or
  yogurt (I use low-fat)

1 cup sliced green
  onions (white and
  green parts)

1/2 tsp ground cumin
  or cumin powder

4 cups (about 1 lb)
  shredded cheddar or
  Monterey Jack cheese
  (2 cups for filling; 2
  cups for topping)

12 corn tortillas

1 can (10 oz) (or 1 pkg
  – follow directions)
  enchilada sauce

black olives for filling
  and/or garnish

shredded or ground
  chicken, beef or pork
  for filling (optional)

Blend the sour cream, most of the green onion,
cumin and 2 cups of the cheese and optional
ingredients if desired.

Dip the tortillas in the enchilada sauce and lay 6
across the bottom of an 8-inch by 10-inch
ungreased baking dish. Place the filling on top of
the tortillas. Dip the remaining 6 tortillas in
enchilada sauce and lay them over the filling.
Pour any remaining sauce on top.

Sprinkle the top with the rest of the cheese and
the remaining green onion.

Bake uncovered in a 375°F
oven for 20 minutes.

Serves about 6.

WOMEN *to* WOMEN
A Gift of Hope

Veal Scallopini

"This recipe is light and easily prepared, yet special enough for entertaining."

1 lb veal cutlets, cut into
    2-inch squares

2 cups crushed canned
    tomatoes

1/2 cup white wine

1/4 cup olive oil

flour to coat

1 tsp salt

1/2 tsp parsley

1/2 tsp oregano

1 - 2 cans (10 oz each)
    mushrooms, drained

thin egg noodles

Coat veal with flour, and shake on seasonings. Brown veal in olive oil in a skillet.

Stir in remaining ingredients. Cover and simmer for approximately 30 minutes.

Serve over cooked egg noodles. Enjoy!

Lyn McLeod, MPP

Member of the Provincial Parliament and Leader of the Ontario Liberal Party
Thunder Bay, Ontario, Canada

"As a woman and a mother of four daughters, I appreciate the work being done by women across Canada to turn the hope of defeating breast cancer into more and more of a reality."

WOMEN *to* WOMEN
A Gift of Hope

Marilyn Beck

Syndicated Hollywood columnist, TV commentator, and reporter
Beverly Hills, California, U.S.A.

"This project is particularly special to me, as a survivor of breast cancer."

Marilyn Beck's Baked Chicken

"My grandchildren love it."

2 envelopes Lipton onion soup mix

3/4 cup fine dry bread crumbs

1 medium broiler-fryer chicken, cut into parts

1/2 cup mayonnaise

Preheat oven to 400°F.

Place soup mix and bread crumbs in a large plastic food bag and shake to blend. Brush chicken on all sides with mayonnaise. Place one piece of chicken in bag at a time; close tightly and shake until coated. Place chicken on rack in broiler pan and bake 40 to 45 minutes, or until golden brown and tender.

Serves 4.

WOMEN *to* WOMEN
A Gift of Hope

Ice Box Rolls, from Joanne Woodward. See page 21.
Spinach Stuffed Manicotti, from Sylvie Fréchette. See page 114.

Sharon's Enchilada Lasagna, from Sharon Hampson. See page 118.

Italian Country Chicken

"Very tasty and quick, and it looks so good!"

3 tbsp olive oil

1 large onion, cut into eighths

2 cloves garlic, minced

1 lb boneless, skinless chicken breast halves, cut into strips

1-1/2 jars (6 oz each) marinated artichoke hearts, drained

1 jar (7 oz) roasted red bell peppers, undrained

1/2 cup pitted black olives

salt and pepper to taste

3/4 lb tricolour fusilli, freshly cooked

freshly grated parmesan cheese to taste

Judith Forst, OC

Opera singer
Port Moody, British Columbia, Canada

Heat oil in heavy, large skillet over medium heat. Add onion and garlic and cook until translucent, stirring occasionally, about 10 minutes.

Add chicken and stir until cooked through, about 8 minutes. Mix in artichoke hearts with liquid, peppers with liquid, and olives, and heat through. Season with salt and pepper.

Pour over pasta and toss well. Serve, passing parmesan separately.

Serves 6 to 8.

Honey-Basil Chicken
Renamed by me
"Soupir au miel"

4 whole chicken legs,
  skinned

1/4 tsp salt

freshly ground black
  pepper to taste

1 tbsp safflower oil

1/2 tbsp unsalted butter

2 tbsp honey

2 tbsp unsalted chicken
  stock

2 cloves garlic, thinly
  sliced

30 - 40 fresh basil leaves

Preheat oven to 400°F.

Cut a piece of aluminum foil 1-foot square for each leg. Sprinkle the legs with the salt and pepper.

Heat the oil and butter in a skillet over medium heat, then brown the legs for about 2 minutes on each side.

Put a leg in the middle of each foil square, and drizzle 1-1/2 tsp of the honey and 1-1/2 tsp of the stock over each one. Lay a quarter of the garlic slices on each piece, cover with a loose layer of the basil leaves, and wrap the foil snugly over the top. Put the foil packages on a baking sheet and set it in the oven.

After 30 minutes, remove a foil package from the oven and unwrap it carefully to preserve the juices. Test for doneness by piercing the thigh with the tip of a sharp knife. If the juices run clear, it is done. If necessary, return the leg to the oven and bake about 5 minutes more.

To serve, undo each package and transfer the legs to a platter. Remove any garlic or basil that sticks to the foil, and put them back on the chicken. Pour the collected juices from the foil packages over the legs.

Serves 4.

Germaine Beaulieu

Nicole Brossard

Poet and novelist
Outremont, Québec, Canada

"Light spinning what is at stake." – from Mauve Desert, *a novel.*

Phyllis Diller's Chicken Charisma

6 boneless, skinless
chicken breasts

lots of butter

1/4 lb fresh mushrooms,
sliced not too thin
(about 1/4 inch)

3 small cans (or 2 large
cans) artichoke hearts

5 cups (approx.) chicken
stock or bouillon

white wine to taste

salt and pepper to taste

Sauté breasts in butter until brown. Remove the breasts from the pan and put in a baking dish.

Add more butter to the skillet in which you just browned the breasts. Add fresh mushrooms and sauté.

Sprinkle mushrooms over the chicken in the baking dish. Place artichoke hearts with chicken ARTISTICALLY in baking dish (allow 2 hearts per person).

In the skillet where you sautéed the mushrooms, add flour to the drippings, plus chicken stock (or bouillon) to make gravy. (Makes about 4 cups of gravy. If you don't have enough drippings for this, add 1 can of chicken gravy.)

Add white wine, salt and pepper to taste. Add NO GARLIC.

Pour gravy over the entire casserole. Cover and bake about 1 hour at 350°F, until chicken breasts are tender. Uncover the casserole the last 15 minutes of baking.

Phyllis Diller

Comedienne, writer, pianist
Los Angeles, California, U.S.A.

Chicken in a Sweet Red Pepper Sauce

"This recipe is adapted from *Madhur Jaffrey's Indian Cookery*. It is easy and delicious, and the dish is beautiful to look at. Serve it with basmati rice."

6 skinless single chicken breasts

1 onion, peeled and coarsely chopped

1 cube (1 inch) ginger, coarsely chopped

3 cloves garlic, peeled

1 lb sweet red pepper, peeled and coarsely chopped

1 tbsp ground cumin

2 tsp ground coriander

1/2 tsp ground turmeric

pinch (or to taste) cayenne

2 tsp salt

4 tbsp vegetable oil

1/2 - 1 cup water

2 tbsp lemon juice

1/2 tsp coarsely ground black pepper

Cut chicken breasts in half portions and remove visible fat.

In food processor fitted with steel blade, put onion, ginger, peppers, cumin, coriander, turmeric, cayenne and salt. Blend until you have a rough paste.

Heat oil in a heavy saucepan over medium heat. When hot, add red pepper paste. Stir and fry for 10 to 12 minutes, or until oil forms tiny bubbles around sides of the pan.

Add chicken with water, lemon juice and black pepper. Stir to mix, and bring to a boil. Turn heat to low and cook, stirring occasionally, for 20 to 25 minutes, or until chicken is tender.

Serves 6.

Donna Nebenzahl

Editor and writer
Montréal, Québec, Canada

"Breast cancer activists have taught us how much can be accomplished by women working together. I am happy to help a cause as important as fundraising for research."

Elegant Chicken

"It's so easy. This can be made and kept warm and served with sauce when ready."

Chicken Mixture

2 tbsp all-purpose flour

1/8 tsp salt

pinch pepper

1/8 tsp paprika

1 tbsp hard margarine (butter browns too fast)

4 boneless chicken breast halves

Hazelnut Sauce

1 cup sliced fresh mushrooms

1/2 cup white wine (or de-alcoholized wine)

1/2 (10 oz) can condensed cream of mushroom soup

1/4 tsp garlic powder

2 tbsp sliced toasted hazelnuts

WOMEN to WOMEN
A Gift of Hope

Combine flour, salt, pepper and paprika in a saucer. Mix. Place in a paper bag.

Melt margarine in frying pan. Coat chicken with flour mixture, shaking 2 or 3 pieces at a time in the bag. Cook and brown chicken until no pink remains. Remove to serving bowl. Keep warm.

In same frying pan, add mushrooms and wine. Stir to loosen brown bits. Boil gently for 3 to 4 minutes to soften mushrooms and reduce liquid.

Stir in soup, garlic powder and hazelnuts. Return to a boil. Pour over chicken.

Serves 4.

Jean Paré

Author and publisher of the Company's Coming *cookbook series*
Edmonton, Alberta, Canada

"I'm just an ordinary homemaker who followed her father's advice: 'Get going and do it!'"

Raspberry Chicken

"Low-fat and low-calorie, yet tastes delicious."

5 oz raspberry
    spreadable fruit

1/2 cup unsweetened
    pineapple juice
    concentrate

1/4 cup soy sauce, low
    sodium

2 tbsp rice vinegar

1/2 tsp chili powder

1/2 tsp garlic powder

1/2 cup fresh raspberries

1/2 cup finely chopped
    fresh basil

2 lbs fresh, boneless,
    skinless chicken breast
    halves

Blend all ingredients together and pour over chicken or fish. Let marinate for several hours before cooking.

Serves 8.

Raspberry Chicken is pictured on page 155.

Sela Ward

Television and movie actress, and star of the television series
Sisters
Beverly Hills, California, U.S.A.

WOMEN *to* WOMEN
A Gift of Hope

Upside Down Spicy Bird

"This recipe will work for chicken, duck or goose."

1 chicken, duck or goose

1 medium onion, finely chopped

1 small red pepper, finely chopped

3 stalks celery, finely chopped

1 tsp (or to taste) red pepper flakes

1/2 cup soy sauce

1/2 cup lemon juice

1/2 cup water

1 tsp crushed rosemary

Skin the bird and place it breast down in a large casserole with high sides. Make sure the opening is facing upwards.

Put the finely chopped onion, red pepper and celery in the cavity.

In a bowl, mix the soy sauce, lemon juice, water, red pepper flakes and rosemary. Pour 3/4 of the mixture into the cavity, and the rest on top of the bird.

Bake covered for 1 hour (or longer if it is a large bird) at 375°F or medium oven. Then uncover and baste. Cook in a hot oven for another 40 minutes, basting a couple of times.

Serve on rice, potatoes or noodles.

If desired, rescue the bird from the broth, remove fat and make gravy. The flavour is strong and zesty.

For larger gatherings, make two or three birds and place on a platter in pieces. Pour thickened gravy over the meat and garnish with fresh tomatoes and cucumbers.

Anne Wheeler

Film director and producer
Ganges, British Columbia, Canada

WOMEN to WOMEN
A Gift of Hope

Creamy Lemon Chicken

"This is my favourite recipe because it's delicious, light, and very easy to make."

6 boneless, skinless chicken breasts

1/2 tsp salt (omit if using salted stock)

1/4 tsp freshly ground black pepper

2 tbsp corn oil margarine

2/3 cup defatted chicken stock

2 tbsp dry sherry

1 tbsp grated lemon zest

2 tbsp freshly squeezed lemon juice

1 tbsp cornstarch

1 cup evaporated skim milk (canned)

1/4 cup freshly grated parmesan cheese, preferably imported

WOMEN to WOMEN
A Gift of Hope

Remove all visible fat from chicken, and sprinkle evenly with salt (if using) and pepper. In a large skillet over medium heat, bring margarine and stock to a boil. Add chicken and cook, turning once or twice, just until chicken is no longer pink, about 6 to 10 minutes.

Transfer chicken to an ovenproof serving dish.

To skillet, add sherry, zest and lemon juice. Add cornstarch to milk. Mix well with a wire whisk, and gradually add to skillet. Cook, stirring constantly, until mixture comes to a boil and thickens.

Pour sauce over chicken. Sprinkle with cheese, and broil until golden brown.

Makes 6 half-breast servings.

Jeanne Jones

Syndicated columnist and author of 30 cookbooks
La Jolla, California, U.S.A.

"I wish you great success with your wonderful project."

Glady's Chicken Chili

"Delicious! Simple! Guaranteed to wow your guests!!"

8 oz chopped onion

1/2 jalapeño pepper, washed, seeded and minced

1 tsp canola oil

1 lime (half for juice, half as wedges)

1/2 tsp ground coriander

1 can (14 oz) crushed tomatoes, chopped

1 can (15 - 16 oz) Primo LoSalt white beans, drained and rinsed

4 tbsp non-fat yogurt

2 large garlic cloves, minced

10 sprigs cilantro

8 oz skinless, boneless chicken breast meat

2 tbsp minced red onion

1 tsp cumin

1 cup frozen corn kernels

pepper to taste

Heat pan on high. Reduce to medium and add oil, onion and garlic. Sauté until light brown. Add chicken and brown both sides.

WOMEN to WOMEN
A Gift of Hope

Add jalapeño, coriander, cumin, tomatoes and beans. Reduce heat and simmer until chicken is cooked.

Squeeze 1/2 lime juice into the chili. Stir in corn. Season with pepper. Continue cooking for 5 minutes.

To serve, top chicken with yogurt, red onion and cilantro. Add lime wedge(s).

"As women, we are truly the nurturers of the world, so it is often through our culinary skills that we are able to assure the well-being of our loved ones. And as women, we are threatened daily by the scourge of a breast cancer diagnosis, which ultimately affects us all as a family, as a community and as a country. By educating ourselves and our loved ones about breast cancer, and by supporting initiatives like In Between Dances* *and* Celebrity Lights, *perhaps we won't have to worry about the future health of our children, and perhaps the research funded by these projects will lead us to that desperately needed cure.*

"Pick some flowers, light the candles, share this recipe with someone you love, and let In Between Dances *soothe your souls! Go well and be well ..."*

Jacki Ralph Jamieson

Singer and recording artist, and national volunteer spokeswoman for the Canadian Cancer Society's Breast Cancer Awareness Month
West Vancouver, British Columbia, Canada

*The recording In Between Dances *raised $1 million for breast cancer research in one year. Among other awards for her cancer support work, Jacki Ralph Jamieson was awarded the 1996 Medal of Courage by the Canadian Cancer Society.*

Sheila's Screaming Hot Chili

"This is easy to make, it is a great meal, and it leaves you more time to enjoy the company of your friends and family."

1 cup chopped onions

1/4 cup chopped green pepper

1 clove garlic, crushed

oil or butter to sauté

1 lb ground beef

3 tbsp (yes, 3 tablespoons!) chili powder

1/4 tsp black pepper

1/2 tsp cayenne pepper

1 large can (28 oz) tomatoes

1 can (5-1/2 oz) tomato paste

1 large can (19 oz) red kidney beans

In a large saucepan, sauté garlic, onions and green pepper in oil or butter. Add ground beef and cook until brown. Add remaining ingredients, except kidney beans. Cover and simmer for 1-1/2 hours.

Add kidney beans and simmer for 15 more minutes.

Serve. Enjoy.

Of course, this recipe can be doubled or tripled ...

Hon. Sheila Copps, MP

Member of Parliament, Deputy Prime Minister and Minister of Canadian Heritage
Hamilton, Ontario, Canada

WOMEN *to* WOMEN
A Gift of Hope

Creole Ham

"I got this out of a Southern cookbook about 1955 or 1956, and I've used it for special occasions ever since then – everyone always expects me to do the ham. When it's done it has a really nice flavour to it."

1 half fresh whole ham (7 - 10 lbs) with the bone in

3 bay leaves, crushed

1 tsp whole peppercorns

1 cup red wine

4 cloves garlic, crushed

1 onion, chopped

paprika to taste

1 tsp Worcestershire sauce

salt and pepper to taste

1/2 tsp garlic powder

In a bowl, combine the bay leaves, peppercorns, wine, cloves of garlic, onion, paprika and Worcestershire sauce. Cover and refrigerate overnight.

A couple of hours before cooking, put the ham in the marinade. Add salt and pepper and garlic powder to taste. Marinate for a couple of hours, then reserve the marinade to use as a baste.

Bake the ham at 325°F for about 1-1/2 hours, until it's done through to the bone. Baste often with the marinade.

Rosemary Brown, OC

Human rights activist and feminist
Vancouver, British Columbia, Canada

Everything nourishes what is strong already.

Jane Austen

Nobody has ever measured, not even poets,
how much the heart can hold.

Zelda Fitzgerald

Firelight

Delicious after-dinner indulgences

WOMEN to WOMEN
A Gift of Hope

Karen Kain's Trifle

Robert Nelson

Karen Kain, CC, LLD, LLT

Principal Dancer,
The National Ballet
of Canada
Toronto, Ontario, Canada

2 cups frozen blueberries, thawed

4 cups individually frozen strawberries, thawed

1 lb pound cake, cubed

1/2 cup sherry

1/4 cup sugar

1/2 cup slivered almonds, toasted

2-1/2 - 3 cups vanilla custard, bought or homemade

1 cup whipping cream

2 tbsp sifted icing sugar

1/4 tsp vanilla

Line a 3-quart glass dish with half of the cubes of pound cake. Sprinkle with half the sherry.

Drain thawed strawberries and blueberries. Purée 2 cups strawberries with sugar. Pour half this purée over soaked cake, then sprinkle half the strawberries and blueberries on top. Spread with half the custard and sprinkle half the toasted almonds on top. Repeat layers.

Cover with plastic wrap and refrigerate several hours or overnight.

Whip the cream, icing sugar and vanilla until soft peaks form. Spread over trifle. Garnish with fresh berries if desired.

Serve 10 to 12.

Karen Kain's Trifle is pictured on page 156.

WOMEN to WOMEN
A Gift of Hope

Carroll Baker's Homemade Grape-nuts™ Ice Cream

"This recipe has been in my family for generations."

3 cans evaporated milk

1-1/2 cups half-and-half

4 eggs

1 cup sugar

1/4 cup Grape-nuts™

pinch salt

1 tbsp vanilla

Mix together until frothy.

Place in ice cream maker, and follow directions of individual machine.

Carroll Baker

Country music recording artist, songwriter and television performer
Guelph, Ontario, Canada

"I am honoured to be a part of this worthy endeavour. Having lost an aunt and a cousin to breast cancer, it is imperative that this deadly disease be wiped out."

Madame Jacob's Oranges Orientales

"From a Brussels hostess. Easy, quick, can be prepared well in advance, light ... diners never leave so much as a drop on their plates."

6 large navel oranges

1 cup sugar

1/2 cup water

1/3 cup currant jelly

2 - 3 tbsp kirsch

slivered almonds
    for garnish

(Mme Jacob always used candied violets, but those are hard to find)

Remove the zest from half the oranges. (A zester with little holes on the end makes this easy.) Put the zest in a small saucepan with water to cover, and boil for 5 minutes. Drain and reserve.

With a serrated knife, peel the oranges, removing the white pith and membrane. Cut each in half at its equator. Then slice each half horizontally into 3 disks. Reform the halves. (This makes it easier to eat.) Place flat side down in a shallow dish that can go in the refrigerator.

In a saucepan, place water and sugar. Add the reserved orange zest. Boil for 3 minutes. Remove from heat, add kirsch and enough currant jelly to make it a nice, rosy colour. Stir to melt the jelly. Taste and add more kirsch if desired.

Spoon some zests onto each orange half, then pour the syrup over all. Store, covered, in the refrigerator until ready to serve.

To serve, place two halves on each plate. Divide the syrup among the dishes. Garnish each with almonds – or candied violets, if you're lucky enough to know where to find them.

(These are still good the next day, but perhaps not quite up to company standards.)

Serves 6.

Madame Jacob's Oranges Orientales are pictured on page 157.

Polly Clingerman

Author
Locust Grove, Virginia, U.S.A.

"I am delighted to be part of this worthwhile project. I wish you well."

145

Beverly Cleary

*Writer of children's books,
including the* Ramona *series*
Carmel, California, U.S.A.

Beverly Cleary's Handy Dessert

"An altered version of a friend's recipe. It is easy to make, and children love it."

3/4 cup graham cracker crumbs

1 can (13 oz) condensed milk, chilled

3/4 cup sugar

1 banana, mashed

juice of 2 lemons

To make crumbs, put graham crackers in a plastic bag and crush with a rolling pin, or use a blender. Spread half of the crumbs over the bottom of a 9-inch square pan.

Whip chilled condensed milk until stiff. Add sugar, banana and lemon juice. Mix well and spread over the crumbs in the pan. Sprinkle the rest of the crumbs over the mixture, and freeze.

Cut into squares to serve.

Variations

Bits of grated chocolate may be added to the condensed milk, banana and lemon, or crushed fruit that is not too juicy may be substituted for the banana.

"Ramona says 'Yummy!' and can make it herself. The rest of her family enjoys it, too."

Crème Caramel

"It's simple to make, can be done a day ahead, and is both elegant and delicious. (Everyone thinks you worked a lot harder than you did.)"

1 cup sugar, divided in half	3 eggs
2 cups light cream or evaporated milk	pinch salt
	1 tsp vanilla
	fresh fruit for garnish

Caramelize 1/2 cup of the sugar by melting it over medium heat in a heavy pan. Immediately coat the inside of a small baking dish with it.

In a saucepan, heat the 2 cups of light cream (I use canned evaporated milk) until bubbles form around the edges.

Meanwhile, beat together the eggs, the second 1/2 cup sugar, salt and vanilla. Slowly add the hot milk to the egg mixture, and mix. Pour into the dish lined with the caramel.

Place the dish in a pan of hot water and bake in a 325°F oven about 50 minutes, or until a silver knife inserted into the centre comes out clean.

Chill until thoroughly cold, as long as overnight. Then unmold onto a serving plate with raised sides.

May be trimmed with peeled, sliced kiwi fruit, or fresh strawberries or raspberries.

Sharon Butala

Writer
Eastend, Saskatchewan, Canada

"My mother died of breast cancer. Two other close relatives have been stricken with it. It hovers over the rest of us – daughters, nieces, cousins."

No-Bake Strawberry Pie

"I clipped this recipe out of the newspaper 15 years ago and it's been a favourite of mine ever since. Every summer my family and friends beg me to make it. It is not exactly a 'light' recipe, but I've modified it so not a lot of sugar is used. It's easy, it's fast, and mouthwatering on a hot night. It always reminds me of my favourite time of year, summer – a time for friends and family."

1, 9-inch pie shell, baked
OR a graham crust pie shell

1/4 - 3/4 cup granulated sugar (I use very little)

3 tbsp cornstarch

pinch salt

1-1/2 cups water

1 pkg (3 oz) strawberry jelly powder (I use artificially sweetened diet jelly powder)

4 cups sliced fresh strawberries

whipped cream (diet, of course) for garnish

WOMEN to WOMEN
A Gift of Hope

In a saucepan, combine sugar, cornstarch and salt. (A pinch of salt boosts the flavour of less-than-perfect berries.) Gradually add water, stirring well. Cook over medium heat, stirring constantly, until thick and clear, about 5 minutes.

Remove saucepan from heat. Add jelly powder and stir until dissolved, about 3 to 4 minutes. Set aside to cool and thicken.

Wash, hull and quarter berries. Set aside a few for garnishing, and place others in the pie shell. Spoon gelatin mixture over berries, and refrigerate until gelatin is firm, about 2 to 3 hours.

Garnish with whipped cream and reserved berries.

Serves 8.

Substitutions

You can vary the recipe using blueberries or kiwi, or all three fruits together.

No-Bake Strawberry Pie is pictured on page 158.

Joy Malbon

Correspondent, CTV Television Network
Toronto, Ontario, Canada

"I love the idea of a cookbook. What better way to bring people together than our love for good food."

Topless Blueberry Pie

No-Mess Crust

Follow the recipe on the Crisco package for the crust. (I make more than I need for one pie – any remaining dough can be frozen for future use.)

Place dough about the size of a softball or grapefruit between two pieces of waxed paper, and roll out. Remove top wax paper, flip over, and press carefully into pie plate. Remove remaining wax paper.

Bake at 375°F until golden brown (about 20 minutes). Remove from oven and set aside to cool.

Filling

6 cups blueberries

1/2 cup brown sugar

1 tsp cinnamon

1/4 cup apple juice or water

4 tbsp cornstarch

Wash blueberries and let them dry completely.

Simmer 2 cups of the blueberries with the sugar, cinnamon, apple juice or water, until soft. Mash berries to release juice. Remove from heat.

Mix some (about 1/4) of the simmered mixture with the cornstarch in a separate cup. Make sure there are no lumps, then add back into the simmered mixture. Stir constantly over heat until mixture thickens. Remove from heat.

Fold in the remaining 4 cups of fresh blueberries and pour it all into the baked crust. That's it. Pile the berries nice and high ... ummmm!

Linda Lundström

Clothing manufacturer/ designer, and public speaker
Toronto, Ontario, Canada

Aunt Christine's Pie

"Christine MacLennan was my mother's elder sister, a school teacher for many years until she married William Dick and settled down to happy wifedom. Childless, they were the perfect aunt and uncle – generous and indulgent.

"More than two decades ago, my aunt died of breast cancer while still in her 60s, a tragedy that could have been averted had she seen her doctor earlier. It is in her honour that I contribute her recipe, which has been a special family favourite of ours over the years. Aunt Christine's Pie is also a 'light' recipe because its ingredients do not include oil or butter ... although it is true, I should add, that it tastes absolutely splendid slathered with whipped or ice cream!"

1 large egg

3/4 cup granulated
  sugar

1 tsp vanilla (let it spill
  over a bit)

1/2 cup white flour

2 generous tsp baking
  powder

1/4 tsp salt

2/3 cup chopped
  walnuts

1-1/2 cups diced apples
  (any variety, or a
  mixture, although
  cooking apples such as
  Spies are probably
  best)

WOMEN to WOMEN
A Gift of Hope

Beat the egg well and add the sugar and vanilla while continuing to beat (with an electric beater) until foamy.

Sift together the flour, baking powder and salt, and then add to the first mixture, including the walnuts and apples at the same time, so that they are slightly coated with flour as they are incorporated into the batter. This mixing can be done with a large spoon.

Pour into a slightly greased pie plate (you could use one of those low-cal sprays, probably) and bake in a 325°F oven for about 45 minutes, until the crust is firm to the touch and the pie-cake is browned at the edges.

This recipe can be easily doubled, either made in a large pie plate or in two small ones.

It is excellent eaten warm (with cream or without) and just as good cold the next day.

Isabel Huggan

Writer of short stories and teacher of creative writing
Manila, The Philippines, and British Columbia, Canada

"I am very pleased to be asked to take part in the project, and as you can see from the recipe I have chosen, it is something for which I have very strong feelings. Sharing favourite recipes, with all of their quirky attributions, is a fine way to acknowledge the importance not only of food, but of stories as nourishment in our lives."

Anne Boyin

Susan Musgrave

Poet, novelist and columnist
Sidney, British Columbia, Canada

"I love cooking, but few of my favourite recipes are low-fat!!"

Apple-Blackberry Pie in a Bag

"From my mother, Judith Musgrave. The ingredients are easy to come by (in summer and fall), and the fact that the pie is cooked in a bag seems to seal in all the flavours."

1 unbaked pie shell	*1 cup granulated sugar*
5 cups apples, chopped into chunks	*1/2 cup + 2 tbsp flour*
	1/2 tsp cinnamon
2 cups blackberries* (or enough fruit to fill a heaping pie plate)	*2 tbsp lemon juice*
	1/2 cup flour
	1/2 cup very soft butter

*This recipe can be made without blackberries – simply use 7 cups of apples.

Toss fruit in a bowl with 1/2 cup of sugar, 2 tbsp of flour, and cinnamon. Fill pie shell, pile high in the middle. Sprinkle with lemon juice.

Mix remaining sugar, 1/2 cup of flour and butter to make a soft paste. Spread on top of fruit.

Put pie in a large paper bag and close open end (I staple it together). Set on a rack in the centre of the oven, *making sure that the bag is not touching any oven elements.*

Bake for about 1 hour at 400°F. Cool for 5 or 10 minutes before removing from the bag.

WOMEN *to* WOMEN
A Gift of Hope

Raspberry Chicken, from Sela Ward. See page 132.

Karen Kain's Trifle. See page 142.

Madame Jacob's Oranges Orientales, from Polly Clingerman. See page 144.

No-Bake Strawberry Pie, from Joy Malbon. See page 148.

Extra-Moist Chocolate Cake, from Carolyn Waldo. See page 163.
Chocolate-Dipped Strawberries, from Sandie Rinaldo. See page 59.

159

Coconut Cake (Mother's), from Jane Urquhart. See page 166.

The World's Best Sponge Cake

"This recipe came from my Mum, Kay West of Fredericton. It was always my birthday cake. It's easy to memorize, simple to make, and useful in trifles and fairly exotic creations when used with fruit and cream or maple syrup or ice cream. Besides, my Mother won prizes with it."

"I always double this." – Kay West

3 eggs

1 cup sugar

1 cup flour

1 huge tsp baking powder

1/2 tsp salt

few drops vanilla

few drops almond

5 tbsp boiling water

Beat eggs and sugar until thick.

Stir together flour, baking powder and salt. Sift. Add to egg and sugar. Add vanilla and almond. Add boiling water, beating after each spoonful.

Bake 30 minutes in a 10-inch tube pan in a 350°F oven.

Mary Francis Pratt

Artist

St. John's, Newfoundland, Canada

"Since much of my work has been inspired by food, I'm especially pleased to be included in this book."

WOMEN *to* WOMEN
A Gift of Hope

Michelle Wright

Arista recording artist and
songwriter
Nashville, Tennessee, U.S.A.

"I guess when you boil it down, the
message is that you'll find happiness
as long as you don't quit growing,
searching, challenging yourself – and
listening to your heart."

Poppy Seed Cake

"A family recipe."

1/4 lb butter	*1/2 cup poppy seeds*
1 cup sugar	*3/4 cup milk*
2 eggs, separated	*1-3/4 cups flour*
1 tsp vanilla	*2 tsp baking powder*

Soak the poppy seeds in the milk.

Cream butter. Add sugar slowly, creaming well. Add egg yolks and beat again until light and fluffy.

Sift the flour with the baking powder.

Beat egg whites until stiff.

Add the poppy seeds and milk to the butter mixture. Beat smooth. Fold in the egg whites.

Bake in greased layer-cake tins at 350°F for 30 minutes.

The layers may be stacked together with cream filling and topped with chocolate icing, if desired, or served plain.

WOMEN *to* WOMEN
A Gift of Hope

Extra-Moist Chocolate Cake

"It's my favourite recipe because it's very moist and chocolately."

1 pkg chocolate cake mix (e.g., devil's food)

1 large pkg chocolate pudding (not instant)

1 cup sour cream

1/2 cup warm water

1/2 cup oil

4 eggs

1 cup chocolate chips

Mix everything together, and fold in chocolate chips. Bake in a bundt pan or a 9-inch by 13-inch pan. Bake for 45 to 55 minutes at 350°F. Enjoy.

Extra-Moist Chocolate Cake is picture on page 159.

Carolyn Waldo

Olympic double gold medallist in synchronized swimming, and Sportscaster for CJOH-TV, Ottawa
Ottawa, Ontario, Canada

WOMEN *to* WOMEN
A Gift of Hope

The Birthday Cake

"This recipe has never been published. It comes from my grandmother – it's a century old! It's my favourite because of its spectacular appearance – very festive – to say nothing of flavour ... and no fat. Delicious."

Lemon Layer Cake

3 eggs

1 cup granulated sugar

1-1/2 cups Swans Down flour (sifted)

2 heaping tsp baking powder

1/8 tsp salt

3 tbsp water

OR 2 tbsp water + 1 tbsp lemon juice

Prepare 2 layer-cake tins, lining sides and bottoms with wax paper. Allow the wax paper to stick up about 1 inch above the edges of the tins.

Beat eggs, adding sugar gradually until stiff or in peaks. Add salt. Add sifted flour and baking powder. Don't overmix. Add liquid. Divide cake batter equally into cake tins. Bake in a 350°F oven for 20 to 25 minutes. Layers are ready for filling when they are medium cool.

WOMEN to WOMEN
A Gift of Hope

Lemon Filling

3 egg yolks	3/4 cup granulated sugar
juice of 1 lemon	1 cup water
1/4 cup grated lemon rind	3 tbsp cornstarch

Mix together in a double boiler until smooth and cooked. Cool.

Remove the cakes from the tins. Cut the cakes in half, making four pieces and three layers to be filled. Spread the lemon filling on the layers. Allow to cool completely.

Frosting

3 egg whites	1/2 tsp cream of tartar
1 cup granulated sugar	1/4 tsp salt
3 tbsp water	

Beat whole mixture in a double boiler for 7 minutes. Add pink colouring. Beat until frosting stands in peaks. Ice the tops and sides when the cake is filled and completely cooled.

Happy Birthday!

Elizabeth Bradford Holbrook,
CM, RCA, OSA, SSC

Artist, wife, mother, cook and senior horse-show judge
Dundas, Ontario, Canada

"I think this is a very interesting project."

Coconut Cake (Mother's)

"I believe there is no mention of coconut in the ingredients because, as my husband Tony says, Grannie didn't like coconut."

Mamie Morse, from her mother, Mary Kick. Always made for birthdays, c. 1880s.

Cake

2/3 cup butter	3 cups pastry flour
2 cups granulated sugar	4 tsp baking powder
4 egg yolks	pinch salt
4 egg whites, beaten stiff	1 cup milk
	1 tsp vanilla

Start with the butter in a bowl. Add sugar gradually, stirring constantly. Add the yolks of the 4 eggs and beat until thick and lemon tinted.

Sift together flour, baking powder and salt. Add this alternately to the first mixture, along with the milk. Add vanilla and fold in the whites of the 4 eggs, beaten stiff.

Bake for 25 to 30 minutes in a quick oven.*

Frosting

2 cups granulated sugar	2 egg whites, beaten stiff
1/4 tsp cream of tartar	1/2 tsp vanilla
1/2 cup boiling water	

Stir the sugar, cream of tartar and boiling water over the fire until the sugar is dissolved and the boiling point is reached. Then wash down the side of the

Women to Women
A Gift of Hope

pan (to remove sugar crystals), cover and let boil 2 minutes.

Uncover and continue boiling until syrup spins a thread.

Pour syrup in a fine stream onto the white of the 2 egg whites, beaten stiff. Dry beat constantly, adding vanilla. Beat until cool enough to spread.

*Takes 1 hour if baked in the long pan.

"This is a recipe handwritten by my husband's grandmother, a woman I never met but someone I feel very close to, not only because of all the things my husband has told me about her, but also because I had the audacity to base one of the characters in my first novel on her.

"One of the things that I love about this recipe is its intimacy. She explains at the top of the list of ingredients that her mother always made this cake for birthdays. I imagine, therefore, a combination of daylight, probably sunlight, and birthday candlelight. It certainly wouldn't be electric light, because my husband's grandmother was born in 1879, and the birthdays in question would probably have been hers as a child.

"Another intimate touch comes at the end of the recipe, where she announces to the reader that the cake 'Takes one hour if baked in the long pan.' Since this family lived for several generations in the same house, she assumes that whoever reads the recipe in the future (i.e., if she is not around to give instructions) will know exactly which long pan she is referring to. I also find lines such as 'until syrup spins a thread' to be very poetic."

Coconut Cake is pictured on page 160.

Tony Urquhart

Jane Urquhart

Novelist
Wellesley, Ontario, Canada

"I think your book is a wonderful idea, and I wish you every success with it."

Marble Mocha Cheesecake

"Fabulous light, creamy dessert. Now you can have your cake and eat it too!!"

Crust

1-1/2 cups chocolate wafer crumbs

2 tbsp granulated sugar

2 tbsp water

1 tbsp margarine or butter

Filling

1-2/3 cups 5% ricotta cheese

1/3 cup light cream cheese, softened

3/4 cup granulated sugar

1 egg

1/3 cup light sour cream or 2% yogurt

1 tbsp all-purpose flour

1 tsp vanilla

1-1/2 tsp instant coffee granules

1-1/2 tsp hot water

3 tbsp semi-sweet chocolate chips, melted

1 tbsp water

WOMEN to WOMEN
A Gift of Hope

Preheat oven to 350°F. Spray an 8-inch springform pan with vegetable spray.

Melt chocolate in the microwave on defrost, or in a double boiler, along with water. Stir until smooth.

Combine chocolate crumbs, sugar, water and margarine. Mix thoroughly. Press into bottom and up sides of springform pan.

In a large bowl or food processor, beat together the ricotta cheese, cream cheese, sugar, egg, sour cream, flour and vanilla until well blended. Dissolve coffee granules in hot water; add to batter and mix until incorporated.

Pour batter into springform pan and smooth top. Drizzle melted chocolate on top. Swirl knife or spatula through the chocolate and batter several times to create marbling.

Bake for 35 to 40 minutes; centre will be slightly loose. Let cool, and refrigerate several hours before serving.

Substitutions

Graham crackers or other cookie crumbs can be used for the crust. If instant coffee is unavailable, use 2 tsp of prepared strong coffee.

Make ahead

Bake as far ahead as two days, and keep refrigerated. Freeze for up to six weeks.

Rose Reisman

International cookbook author
Willowdale, Ontario, Canada

"Having sold more than 500,000 copies of books and raised more than $500,000 for breast cancer research, I hope to continue raising funds for breast cancer research, treatment and prevention through the 'simple' purchase of a cookbook."

Nothing in life is to be feared.
It is only to be understood.

Marie Curie

Do not wait for leaders;
do it alone, person to person.

Mother Teresa

Inner Light

Nourishment for the heart and soul

WOMEN *to* WOMEN

A Gift of Hope

Seeking "The Light" Through Fasting

Source: "Every holy book of every religion, plus all books on alternative health and healing."

"I love good food, but after all is said and done (and eaten!), nothing brings me closer to 'The Light', to my real self and to God, than fasting."

A fast can be even one day – even one morning!

Don't eat. Sip water. Sit quietly.

See a laser beam of light entering from the top of your head and infusing your whole body.

The Light be with you.

Emilia Davidson

Teresa Stratas

A seeker of "The Light"
New York, New York, U.S.A.

"Thirty-five years of leading roles with the Metropolitan Opera ... working in the Home for the Dying in India and caring for AIDS babies in Romania ... this is perhaps not a typical response, but since the light is of such interest in my personal journey, I thought I should respond."

Do not follow where the path may lead.
Go instead where there is no path and leave a trail.

Muriel Strode

Life shrinks or expands
in proportion to one's courage.

Anaïs Nin

The Project

Acknowledgements, indexes and ordering details

Many Thanks

Individual Contributors

Celebrity Lights is the product of the talents, hard work and generosity of many people. A heartfelt **Thank you** to you all for your wonderful gifts to this project.

Bob Adshead

Trudy Alexander

Gillian Anderson

Heather Anderson

Dr. Mary-Wynne Ashford

Bev Bain

Barb Baird

Elizabeth Baird

Carroll Baker

Peter Battistoni

Marilyn Beck

The Best of Bridge Women

Bonnie Blair

Hon. Ethel Blondin-Andrew

Elizabeth Bradford
   Holbrook

Lorne Braithwaite

Karen Brimacombe

Ray Brittain

Nicole Brossard

Rosemary Brown

Nicole Brugger

Pam Bryson

Nina Budman

Sharon Butala

Brenda Cairns

Cherie M. Calbom

June Callwood

The Rt. Hon. Kim Campbell

Ruth Carrier

Michael Carroll

Samantha Carruthers

Carolyn Chase

Liz Chase

Shelley Chase

Wei Chen

Aline Chrétien

Peter Christle

Adrienne Clarkson

Beverly Cleary

Diane Clement

Polly Clingerman

Hillary Clinton

Holly Cole

Joan Collins

Kelly Collins

Patricia Conroy

Hon. Anne C. Cools

Hon. Sheila Copps

Geri Cox

Sara Craig

Carrie Crowe

Kelly Cunningham

Christine Curtis

Barry Dash

Donna Dash

Ron Dash

Robert Dees

Phyllis Diller

Kim Douglas

Michael Downs

Leah Du Fresne, In Memory

Sandy Dulmadge

Brian Dunn

Chris Dunn

David Earl

Dorothy Earl

Lindy Edgett

Tracy Eloson

Hon. Joyce Fairbairn

Mary Lou Fassel

Dr. Sylvia Fedoruk

Don Fender

Iola Feser

Frances Fisher

Delores Ford

Josie Forrest

Judith Forst

Sylvie Fréchette

Hilary Godley

Bruce Gordon

Mary Halpen

Sharon Hampson

Marjorie Harris

Pauline Hill

Isabel Huggan

Monica Hughes

Valerie Hunt

Linda Jacobson

Susanne Jakobson

Jacki Ralph Jamieson

Mary-Jane Jessen

Jeanne Jones

Annabelle Jones-Litton

Karen Kain

Joanne Kates

Mary Kay Ash

Geraldine Kenney-Wallace

Diana Kershaw

Elsie Kershaw

Frank Kershaw

Chris Kindratsky

Adella Krall

Diana Krall

Don Kraushar

Karen Lange

Vicki Lawrence Schultz

Lisa Leighton

Janet Lewis

Catherine Lien

Peter Luedke

Valerie Luedke

Veronica Luedke

Wilf Luedke

Linda Lundström

Fiona MacDonald

Hon. Flora MacDonald

Jean MacDonald

Gayle MacKay

Hon. Alexa McDonough

John McGeachy

Morley McKeachie

Shelley McKeachie

Loreena McKennitt

Shawney McCutcheon

Sarah McLachlan

Hon. Audrey McLaughlin

Cathy McLellan

Lyn McLeod

Sarah McNaughton

Colin McTaggart

Cathy Madill

Joy Malbon

Nancy Marino

Kathy Mattea

Judith Maxwell

Deborah Melanson

Shirley Mesbur

Joy Metcalfe

Helen Miles

Garry Miller

Vicky Miller
Jack Milliken
Barbara Mills
Lorraine Monk
Mila Mulroney
Anne Murray
Susan Musgrave
Dr. Helen K. Mussallem
Donna Nebenzahl
Sheila Nelson
Michael James O'Connor
Evelyn O'Rourke
Bob Palmer
Marlene Palmer
Jean Paré
Dale Partridge
Jody L. Paterson
Patricia Patkau
Pat Patten
Terry Patterson
Deni Pavan
Jane Penner
Cassandra Peterson
Dini Petty
Mary Francis Pratt
Valerie Pringle
Susan Raduy
Heather Rankin

Rose Reisman
Traci Reynolds
Sandie Rinaldo
Barry Ringstead
Mel Rivet
David Roach
Bonnie Robertson
Val Robinson
Peter Robson
Monda Rosenberg
Marg Ruttan
Vicki Ryall
Marnie Ryder
Buffy Sainte-Marie
John Salus
Darlene Schmidt
Regina Schrambling
Nola Sedgewick
Carol Shields
Sandra Shinnan
Carrie Shoen
Jane Siberry
Luc Simard
Judy Simpson
Linda Smith
Sonja Smits
Erik Stallknecht
Kim Stallknecht

Doreen Stinson
Sandra Stone
Teresa Stratas
Lee Taylor
Sue Taylor
Brenda Thompson
Roberta Tower
C.J. Tripp
Jane Urquhart
Lorna Vander Haeghe
Arla Vander Voet
Carolyn Waldo
Pamela Wallin
Cecilia Walters
Lisa Walters
Sela Ward
Kim Warner
Jack Weiser
Karen Welds
Anne Wheeler
Vanna White
Wendy Williams
Joan Wilson
Katherine Woodhouse
Wendy Woodley
Joanne Woodward
Colette Wright
Michelle Wright

Major Sponsors

We could not have put together a project of the magnitude of *Celebrity Lights* - and been able to offer the book for the low price of $15 - without significant financial help. We are very grateful to the special donors below for their major financial contributions to *Celebrity Lights.*

Cambridge Shopping Centres Ltd., Toronto, Ontario

Island Paper Mills Co. Ltd., New Westminster, British Columbia

Neo Graphics Communication Design, Nanaimo, British Columbia

Overwaitea/Save-On Food Stores, Vancouver Island, British Columbia

Estate of William Paulson, In Memory, Victoria, British Columbia

Quadra Printers Ltd., Nanaimo, British Columbia

Royal Bank of Canada, Central Vancouver Island Area, British Columbia

Kim Stallknecht Photography, Vancouver, British Columbia

Watchword Editorial Services, Victoria, British Columbia

Supporting Businesses

We also thank the many retailers and businesses who have supported the *Celebrity Lights* project by purchasing and/or selling books without profit.

A & W Restaurant - Tillicum Mall

Alberni Mall

Anna's Hair Design

A Step Ahead Footwear Inc.

The Bay - Mayfair Shopping Centre

The Bay - Victoria

The Bay - Woodgrove Centre

Bead Street

Bestwick & Partners

Bolen Books

Broughton Square Postal Outlet & Lottery

Cambridge Shopping Centres Ltd.

Can West Shopping Centre

Chatwin Engineering Ltd.

Coast Country Insurance

Comox Centre Mall

Comox Valley Flowers

Compucentre - Nanaimo

Cotton Ginny Plus

Country Club Centre

Country Grocer

Crabtree & Evelyn

Demie's Shoes

Driftwood Mall

Eaton's - Tillicum Mall

Eaton's - Victoria Eaton Centre

Eaton's - Woodgrove Centre

Entrée Lifestyles

Esquimalt Plaza Merchants Association

Eurodown Quilts

Evans Bastion Insurance Agencies Ltd.

Faces & Shear Design

Fanny's Fabrics & Home Accents

Flandangles

Georgia Strait Outfitters

Getting It Write Cards - Gifts - Filofax

Gnomes Kitchens

Hair Razors Salon

Happy Hands Crafts & Gifts

Harbour Park Mall

Hemlock Printers Ltd.

Hillside Centre

His 'n' Hers Jewellers

Ironwood Mall

Jewelry International

J.T. Flair Salon

Just Right Gifts

Ladies Only Fitness

Levesque Securities Inc. -
   Ruby Diamond, CFP

The Levi's Store

McConnon, Bion, O'Connor & Peterson

McMillan College Inc.,
   The Training Centre

Market Square

Marks & Spencer

Marlin Travel - Mayfair Shopping Centre

Marlin Travel - Woodgrove Centre

Mayfair Shopping Centre

Medichair Medical Equipment

Merle Norman

Morguard Investments Limited

Nanaimo Breast Screening Clinic

The Newsrack

Odlum Brown Limited

Overwaitea Foods & Drugs

Pacific Coast Savings Credit Union

The Panhandler

Pastel's Café

Pennington's Wearhouse

Peoples Drug Mart - Fairfield Plaza

Peoples Drug Mart -
   Mayfair Shopping Centre

Pharmasave - Comox Centre Mall

Pharmasave Ltd.

Please Mum - Nanaimo

Ramars Gifts, Bradford Collectibles

Royal Bank of Canada -
   Central Vancouver Island

Royal Bank of Canada -
   Woodgrove Centre

Rutherford Mall

Sassafras - Mayfair Shopping Centre

Save-on Foods

Scizzorhandz

The Smart Book Shop

Split Ends Salon

Stephanies Children's Fashions

Sutton Group Future Realty - Walt Burgess

Tabi International

Thomas Cook Travel at Eaton's

Thunderbird Mall

Town & Country Realty & Insurance

Town & Country Shopping Centre

Trendy Classics Ladies' Designer Fashions

Unique Gifts & Engraving Ltd.

Victoria Centre Screening Mammography Program of B.C.

Victoria Silk 'n Lace Inc.

Visions One Hour Optical Ltd. - Tillicum Mall

Visions One Hour Optical Ltd. - Victoria

Visions One Hour Optical Ltd. - Woodgrove Centre

Wembley Books & Lotto

Wembley Mall

C.D. Wilson & Associates

The Wise Owl

Woodgrove Centre

Woodgrove Knife Shoppe Ltd.

Woolly Gift Shoppe

Work World #101

Thanks to The Bay and to Gnomes Kitchens, both of Woodgrove Centre, Nanaimo, for supplying china, cutlery, serving dishes and accessories for the *Celebrity Lights* photographs. Thanks also to McMillan College, The Training Centre, Nanaimo, British Columbia, for recipe testing and for looking after mail-order fulfillment of the cookbooks.

Reprint Acknowledgements

Every effort has been made to determine the ownership of all recipes from previously published sources submitted to the *Celebrity Lights* project, and to secure the necessary reprint permissions. In the event that an error or omission has been made, the publisher and production team warrant that it has been made inadvertantly, and express regret, but trust that the originating author or publisher will treat its one-time use in this publication as a gift to breast cancer research.

We gratefully acknowledge the publishers and authors listed below for their kind permissions to reprint copyrighted material. All permissions were given free of charge, as a gift to the *Celebrity Lights* project.

Elizabeth Baird, Wild Rice Muffins (page 22)
Reprinted from *Canadian Living's Country Cooking* by Elizabeth Baird. Toronto: Random House of Canada Ltd., ©1991. Reprinted by permission of the publisher.

Sonja Smits, Curried Carrot Soup (page 28)
Adapted from *In Good Time, The Barbra Schlifer Commemorative Clinic Cookbook* by Barbra Schlifer. Toronto: The Barbra Schlifer Commemorative Clinic, ©1986. Reprinted by permission of the clinic.

Hon. Flora MacDonald, Scotch Broth (page 41)
Reprinted from *Company's Coming Soups and Sandwiches* by Jean Paré. Edmonton: Company's Coming Publishing Limited, ©1987. Reprinted by permission of the author/publisher.

Monica Hughes, Spicy Salmon Mold (page 45)
Adapted from "Scottish Salmon Mold" by Jehane Benoit. Book title unknown. Adaptation provided by the contributor.

The Best of Bridge Women (Karen Brimacombe, Mary Halpen, Linda Jacobson, Helen Miles, Val Robinson, Joan Wilson), Santa Fe Salad (page 47)
Reprinted from *That's Trump, More Recipes From The Best of Bridge* by The Best of Bridge Women. Calgary: The Best of Bridge Publishing Ltd., ©1995. Reprinted by permission of the authors/publishers.

Cherie M. Calbom, Ms, CN, Apple-Cinnamon Cabbage Salad (page 50)
From *The Healthy Gourmet* by Cherie M. Calbom. ©1995 Cherie M. Calbom. New York: Clarkson N. Potter, a division of Crown Publishers, Inc. Reprinted by permission of the publisher.

Hon. Anne C. Cools, Antipasto (page 65)
Reprinted from *The Best of Bridge Cookbook* - the red book! by The Best of Bridge Women. Calgary: Best of Bridge Publishing Limited, ©1976. Updated and reprinted by permission of the authors/publishers.

Pamela Wallin, Skordalia (page 68)
Adapted from "Not Mom's Beans" by Regina Schrambling, which first appeared in *Esquire Magazine*, July 1989. New York. Reprinted by permission of the author/copyright holder.

Patricia Patkau, Parsley and Rice Casserole (page 74)
A slight variation on a recipe by this name in *Vegan Delights* by Jeanne Marie Martin. Madeira Park, British Columbia: Harbour Publishing Co. Ltd., ©1993. Reprinted by permission of the publisher.

Judith Maxwell, Chinese Beef with Crisp Vegetables (page 88)
Reprinted from *Rose Reisman Brings Home Light Cooking* by Rose Reisman. Toronto: Robert Rose Inc. Publisher, ©1995. Reprinted by permission of the publisher.

Marg Ruttan, Dilled Orange and Almond Chicken Stir-Fry (page 94)
From *Low Fat, Low Salt, Low Stress* by Marg Ruttan and Lew Miller. To be published in 1997. Printed by permission of the authors.

Joanne Kates, Warm Lentil Salad (page 96)
From *The Joanne Kates Cookbook* by Joanne Kates. New York: Oxford University Press. Provided by the author.

Joan Collins, Pasta Primavera (page 98)
Reprinted from *Joan Collins: My Secrets*, © 1994, Jemstar International Inc. Provided by the author.

Diana Krall, Diana Krall's West Coast Clams (page 106)
   Adapted from "Mussels Provençale" from *MORE Chef on the Run* by Diane Clement.
   Vancouver: Sunflower Publications Ltd., ©1984. Reprinted by permission of the author.

Sylvie Fréchette, Spinach Stuffed Manicotti (page 114)
   Reprinted from *Company's Coming Pasta* by Jean Paré. Edmonton: Company's Coming
   Publishing Limited, ©1990. Reprinted by permission of the author/publisher.

Hon. Ethel Blondin-Andrew, Linguine with Tomatoes and Basil (page 116)
   Reprinted from *The Silver Palate Cookbook* by Julee Rosso & Sheila Lukins. New York:
   Workman Publishing Company, Inc. Copyright ©1979, 1980, 1981, 1982 by Julee Rosso
   and Sheila Lukins. Reprinted by permission of Workman Publishing Company, Inc. All
   rights reserved.

Nicole Brossard, Honey-Basil Chicken (page 124)
   Reprinted from *Healthy Home Cooking: Fresh Ways with Poultry* by the Editors of Time-Life
   Books. Alexandria, VA: Time-Life Books, ©1986. Reprinted by permission of the
   publisher.

Jean Paré, Elegant Chicken (page 130)
   Reprinted from *Company's Coming Chicken, Etc.* by Jean Paré. Edmonton: Company's
   Coming Publishing Limited, ©1995. Reprinted by permission of the author/publisher.

Sela Ward, Raspberry Chicken (page 132)
   Adapted from *Eating By Design* by Carrie Latt Wyatt, Nutritionist. Reprinted by
   permission of the author.

Jeanne Jones, Creamy Lemon Chicken (page 134)
   Reprinted from *Diet for a Happy Heart* by Jeanne Jones. Santa Rosa, California:
   Cole Publishing Group, Inc. ©1988. Reprinted by permission of the publisher,
   Cole Publishing Group, Inc.

Rose Reisman, Marble Mocha Cheesecake (page 168)
   Reprinted from *Rose Reisman's Enlightened Home Cooking* by Rose Reisman. Toronto:
   R. Rose, ©1996. Published as a fundraising project of the National Breast Cancer Fund.
   Reprinted by permission of the author.

Photographs

All photographic images of the contributors in *Celebrity Lights* were obtained and contributed by the celebrities or their representatives, or by the *Celebrity Lights* production team. If identified on the photographs, photographers have been credited beside their work. If a photographer was not identified on a photograph, the publisher and production team express regret, but cannot accept responsibility for material not provided to them.

We gratefully acknowledge the photographers and photography sources listed below, whose work appears as part of the *Celebrity Lights* gift:

Anne Bayin

Germaine Beaulieu

Michael Bedford Photography

Gary Bernstein

Peter Caton/Gerald Campbell Studios

Bruce Davidson

Emika Davidson

Heather Dean

Michael Dismatsek Photography

Ann Elliott-Cutting

George Evanshuk

David Goldner

Denise Grant

Caroline Greyshock

John Hryniuk Photography

Jon Joosten Photography

Dennis Keeley

Michael Lavine/FOX

Andrew MacNaughtan

Milne Photography

Robert Nelson

Terry Patterson

Phillip Smith

Kim Stallknecht

Rick Stewart/Allsport

Roman Tarnovetsky

Malcolm Tweedy

Tony Urquhart

Victoria Times Colonist

George Whiteside

Index by Celebrity

Additional Copies of Celebrity Lights

Additional copies of *Celebrity Lights* are available by mail.

Please copy and complete the form, below, and return it to:

McMillan College
The Training Centre
3371 Shenton Road
Nanaimo, British Columbia
V9T 2H1 Canada

We regret that fax and phone orders cannot be accepted, but all book orders will be processed as quickly as possible. Allow four to six weeks for delivery.

• •

Celebrity Lights *Order Form*

Copies of *Celebrity Lights* are $15.00 each (CDN). Within North America, add $3.00 per copy for shipping and handling. Outside of North America, add $5.00 per copy for shipping and handling. Payment must be in Canadian funds. Please do not mail cash.

Name: _____

Mailing address: _____

_____

Daytime telephone: _____

Please send me _____ copies of *Celebrity Lights*. My payment is by:

❏ cheque   ❏ money order

❏ VISA   Expiry date: _____

Credit card number: _____

Signature: _____

When I stand before God at the end of my life,
I would hope that I would not have
a single bit of talent left, and could say,
"I used everything you gave me."

Erma Bombeck